D1498481

WETHERSFIELD INSTITUTE
Proceedings, 1994

THE EVER-ILLUMINATING WISDOM OF SAINT THOMAS AQUINAS

The Ever-Illuminating Wisdom of St. Thomas Aquinas

Papers Presented at a Conference
Sponsored by the Wethersfield Institute
New York City, October 14, 1994

IGNATIUS PRESS   SAN FRANCISCO

Cover art: *The Triumph of St. Thomas Aquinas*
by Francesco Traini
S. Caterina, Pisa, Italy
Scala/Art Resource, New York

Cover design by Riz Boncan Marsella

Published 1999, Ignatius Press, San Francisco
ISBN 0-89870-749-8
Library of Congress catalogue number 99-73019
Printed in the United States of America ∞

WETHERSFIELD INSTITUTE
STATEMENT OF PURPOSE

The purpose of the Wethersfield Institute is to promote a clear understanding of Catholic teaching and practice, and to explore the cultural and intellectual dimensions of the Catholic Faith. The Institute does so in practical ways that include seminars, colloquies and conferences especially as they pursue our goals on a scientific and scholarly level. The Institute publishes its proceedings.

It is also interested in projects that advance those subjects. The Institute usually sponsors them directly, but also joins with accredited agencies that share our interests.

CONTENTS

Contributors 9

PETER KREEFT:
When Philosophy and Life Are One 11

MARIE I. GEORGE: "Trust Me." "Why Should I?"
Aquinas on Faith and Reason 31

JOHN M. HAAS: The Relationship of Nature and
Grace in Saint Thomas 59

RALPH MCINERNY: Thomas Aquinas and
Moral Relativism 85

RUSSELL HITTINGER: Aquinas and the
Rule of Law 99

RONALD MCARTHUR: Saint Thomas and the
Formation of the Catholic Mind 123

Abbreviations 145

CONTRIBUTORS

MARIE I. GEORGE is an associate professor of philosophy at St. John's University, New York.

JOHN M. HAAS is the president of the National Catholic Bioethics Center in Boston. He was formerly the John Cardinal Krol Professor of Moral Theology at Saint Charles Borromeo Seminary, Philadelphia.

RUSSELL HITTINGER is Warren Professor of Catholic Studies and Research Professor of Law at the University of Tulsa.

PETER KREEFT is a professor of philosophy at Boston College and author of thirty-five books.

RONALD MCARTHUR was the founding president of Thomas Aquinas College, California.

RALPH MCINERNY is a professor of philosophy, the Grace Professor of Medieval Studies, and the director of the Jacques Maritain Center at the University of Notre Dame. He is also the author of the Father Dowling stories and other works.

PETER KREEFT

WHEN PHILOSOPHY
AND LIFE ARE ONE

It is with fear and trembling that I attempt to fulfill the task assigned to me today. For my talk is supposed to be scholarly, but I am not a scholar. I do not have the time to languish in libraries, for six reasons: a wife, four children, and a house. I write my books in the bathtub and on the beach.

A second reason for my fear and trembling is that my talk is supposed to be biographical, but I am not a biographer, or a historian, or a psychologist. Furthermore, Chesterton has already written the best, the definitive popular biography of Saint Thomas, a book two of the greatest Thomist scholars of our century, Étienne Gilson and Anton Pegis, have both called simply the best book ever written about Saint Thomas. The weight of Chesterton's work exceeds mine as vastly as the weight of his body.

In preparing this talk, I toyed for a moment with the theory that my assignment was a joke, that you were hoping for some comic relief. But relief from what? I am the first speaker on the program. Then I thought it must have been desperation that lay behind the assignment, like the desperation of the baseball fanatic at this time of year, with no real World Series available and nothing to do but ask a Little League team to play in a Major League park.

Then I decided to stop playing amateur psychologist and speculating about motives and simply do what we fools and philosophers do best: rush in where angels fear to tread. (No angel has yet written a paper on the Angelic Doctor, I think. . . .)

The main point of my talk will be the amazing unity between Thomas' writings and Thomas' life, between his mind and his personality. There is always some connection, of course; we do not change personalities when we write. But there is seldom such a perfect unity of life and thought as we find in Aquinas, such a seamless garment. He can therefore serve as a model and patron saint to those of us who are also writers or thinkers and who would like to put more of our good thoughts into practice in our lives as well as more of the goodness of life into our thoughts and writings.

Saint Thomas praises Socrates for this integrity in the *Summa Theologiae* III, 42, 4. The article asks about Christ's teaching method, specifically why he never wrote. Thomas, in answer, distinguishes a lower and a higher mode of teaching. The higher mode is teaching with a complete and perfect life. The lower mode needs to supplement the teacher's imperfect life with some writings. Thus the question: Why did Christ write nothing? is answered. But Thomas then adds that among the philosophers this higher mode of teaching is also found in Socrates.

A footnote: Christ did in fact write, on one occasion, but in sand, not on paper. The incident is in John 8, the woman caught in adultery. No one but the Pharisees knows what he wrote; but I will give you my guess. Names. Names the Pharisees would know. Names like Jennifer Flowers, Paula Jones . . .

Socrates also wrote—on stone. He was a stonecutter. I like to think that the wit and irony of God's providence arranged for him to have written the inscription Saint Paul in Acts 17 saw on Mars Hill and referred to in his sermon to the philosophers of Athens, the inscription that functioned as a Gentile John the Baptist, a preparation for the gospel. The inscription said, "TO THE UNKNOWN GOD". Perfectly Socratic.

I select ten themes, ten features I find in both Thomas' life and his work. Each is illustrated by an incident from his life. They are: his absentmindedness, his childlike simplicity, his purity, his silence, his humility, his detachment, his courtesy, his science, his curiosity, and his prayerfulness.

The other characters who enter the quiet drama of his life to illustrate these characteristics are: Saint Louis, King of France; Brother Reginald, his confessor; a prostitute; his fellow students; his teacher, Saint Albert the Great; his mother; a Really Stupid Philosopher named David of Dinant; a donkey; and Jesus Christ.

1. Absentmindedness

There are two opposite reasons for absentmindedness. I know; I am an expert—from experience. Sometimes you are so scatterbrained that you cannot concentrate on any one thing. You have a short attention span. Hyperactive people, "Type A personalities", and people with the most common form of A.D.D. (Attention Deficit Disorder) are like that. Aquinas, like many professors, including myself, was the opposite type: once the attention of this type is fixed on something, it likes to stay there. It hates interruptions. It seems hypo-active: passive, pensive, quiet. This is the opposite form of A.D.D. Many professors I know have this profile—probably because we could not succeed at anything else in the world except academics. Before Plato invented the academy, we would not have survived except as hermits, outcasts, or court jesters.

The well-known incident with Saint Louis illustrates Saint Thomas' single-minded absentmindedness. He was sitting at a banquet table with the king and many V.I.M.P.'s (Very Important Medieval People). All of them had been *chatting*— something people like Saint Thomas are not very good at. He had evidently been doing something else: thinking. For out of the silence there suddenly emerged a crash of his fist on the table and a crash of his voice in the air: "*That* will settle the Manichees!"

Words that emerge from the silence are strong, like trees

with deep roots, or like the sea. Words that emerge only from the noise of other words are like grass, with shallow roots, or like babbling brooks. Babbling brooks are not absentminded. The sea is absentminded. Suddenly—a storm. Great waves, like Thomas' great fist upon the table.

According to the story, King Louis, also a saint and therefore marching to the same divine drummer as Thomas, following the same conductor, though in a different section of the orchestra, played the right note. He immediately whispered to his scribe to take a writing tablet to the absentminded professor and note down the argument against the Manichees that had impressed him so. Thank God for his present mind—and for Aquinas' absent mind. "Absent from the body, present with the Lord."

Of course we need more than professors' arguments, but not less, against the modern Manichees, the despisers of matter, motherhood, flesh, birth, breeding, nature, natural sexual differences, natural intercourse, natural suffering, and natural death; against New Age spirituality and radical feminist resentment at the "prison" of the womb and motherhood, against abstract, fleshless ideologies, against artificial attacks on birth and breeding, against the rape of nature, especially human nature, against the radical redefining of maleness and femaleness, and against the trashing of the quintessentially Christian idea that the cross of suffering and death is noble and dignified and meaningful and not to be Kevorkianized. Sometimes it takes a professor to refute the professors, an absentminded professor to refute an absentminded ideology.

By the way, no one knows what argument occurred to Aquinas that day, but I suspect it was this one, bright and simple as a star, against the Manichean doctrine that some things (matter) are ontologically evil:

Everything that exists is either God the Creator or his creature.

But the Creator is perfectly good, and the deliberate creations of God are all good.

Therefore everything that exists is ontologically good. Only a child or a pure professor would invent such a simple and obvious argument.

Aquinas' absentmindedness was that of Mary in a world of Marthas. There were more Marys in the Middle Ages than there are in the modern world, and more a generation ago than today. Abstraction from the Martha worries, detachment from the many Martha things, is becoming increasingly rare and therefore increasingly necessary not only for sanctity but for sanity.

Aquinas once addressed the Disputed Question of whether the contemplative life or the active life is the more perfect. With Solomonic wisdom, he answered: The mixed life is the most perfect, the most complete, and the most Christlike. Aquinas' absentmindedness coexisted with a busy, active life full of controversy, work, and teaching. Aquinas would heartily approve the saying of José Escrivá, the beatified founder of Opus Dei, that "we must do the works of Martha in the spirit of Mary." He would agree with Plato that complete education includes the world outside the Cave and the world of shadows in the Cave—and with Chesterton that man is neither a mole burrowing in the earth nor a balloon floating in the sky, but a tree with roots planted firmly in the earth and branches reaching into the heavens. In other words, this absentminded professor had his head in the clouds and his feet on the ground—obviously the proper place for both. Not to have one's head in the clouds is to be an intellectual midget.

2. Simplicity

Aquinas was simpleminded. Now what kind of ridiculous saying is that about the greatest theological genius who ever lived? Obviously, by "simpleminded" I do not mean "mentally retarded". I mean exactly the opposite: mentally advanced. When we are first born, we are not simpleminded. The world seems a buzzing, booming confusion. Gradually, we discern order out of chaos, principles guiding events, simplicity holding together complexity in a system, a body. Mental advancement consists largely in moving toward the organic unity, the unity-in-multiplicity, that characterizes our own bodies, or any organic body, and that characterizes the universe—the *uni-versa* —and that characterizes all reality because all reality reflects the unity of its Creator. Unity is a transcendental property of all being, according to Thomistic metaphysics. But we realize this inductively, not deductively; by experience, not by remembering some innate idea, according to Thomistic epistemology. Therefore, combining the premise of Thomistic metaphysics and the premise of Thomistic epistemology, we reach the conclusion that to be simpleminded is to be near the summit of the human mount of intellectual development. Aquinas gave us his sermons on the mount.

Simplemindedness does not exclude complexity and subtlety. It makes it possible, as the soul makes the living body possible. The human body, especially the brain and nervous system, is the most physically complex thing in the known universe, *because* the human soul is the most simple and unified thing in the known universe. That is why it is immortal: having no parts, it can not fall apart.

Thomas' poetry shows his simplemindedness. It constantly rings the changes on a single theme. Its structure is like that of a wheel, each spoke connecting to the center. And the center is Christ, the God-man. Thomas' poetry is unlike his philosophy only in its vocabulary. It shows the same spirit of simplicity, the same artless art of childlike directness and clarity. Three of the qualities Aquinas declared to be essential properties of beauty were harmony or proportion, clarity, and "bright colors". Just what a child would say. And just what Aquinas' poetry is like.

Poetry is a joint effort of head and heart. Aquinas' poetry manifests his simpleheartedness as well as his simplemindedness. Simpleheartedness is even more important than simple-

mindedness. It is the very definition of sanctity. It is what
Kierkegaard meant when he wrote that wonderful title *Purity
of Heart Is to Will One Thing*. It is what our Lady manifested
perfectly with her answer to Mailman Gabriel's invitation to
the spiritual wedding with God: "Yes." *Fiat.* "Be it done to me
according to thy word." And thus our salvation was made possible. It is what Muslims rightly see as the very essence of true
religion—*islam*, total submission to God. It is what William
Law shows us we lack when he writes this devastating diagno-
sis: "If you will examine your own heart in all honesty, you
will inevitably come to the conclusion that there is one and
only one reason why you are not even now a saint. You do
not wholly want to be."

Simplicity of heart is the criterion of sanctity. Thomas had
it. The incident in his life that illustrates this most perfectly
to me comes near its end. He had just finished the treatise
on the Eucharist. Brother Reginald, his friend and confessor,
testified that he saw Thomas alone in the chapel, prone (or as
nearly prone as his rotundity would allow), being addressed by
an audible voice from the crucifix: "You have written well of
me, Thomas. What will you have as your reward?" Thomas'
instant reply was, simply: "Only thyself, Lord."

What humility! And at the same time, what chutzpah, what
moxie! Nothing more and nothing less than God himself. The
audacious simplicity of it! The story brings a lump to my throat
and a tear to my eye every time I tell it—not only because
I, too, long to give him the same answer, but also because I
know that at every minute I continue to fail radically to do the
thing I long to do. For there is a hard word in Thomas' reply.
It is not "thyself", for God's self is infinitely attractive. It is
not even "Lord", though bending the knee to his lordship is a
continual pain for us who have contracted the hereditary dis-
ease of spiritual arthritis. But it is the word "only", the word of
simplicity. It was his word to Martha: "Martha, Martha, you
are worried and anxious because your eyes and your heart are

on many things. Only one thing is necessary. And he stands before you." Thomas, like Mary, simply sat at his feet. That is why the *Summa* is so full of seraphic light. A child is simpler than an adult. Aquinas was a child. He had a child's simple fear: thunderstorms. A natural, innocent fear. He would understand, as we do not, the ancient temptation to believe in many gods and to fear Zeus Thunderer and Poseidon Earth-Shaker. The fear of the gods is not the beginning of wisdom, but it is close to it. The fear of the gods is at least closer to the fear of God than the chummy, chatty informality, popularity, and adjustment to the Kingdom of This World that are recommended to us by so many of our modern religious educators and "experts" and pastoral psychologists and liturgists.

Karl Barth, the great neo-orthodox Protestant theologian, was asked, after his last public lecture, this question: "Professor Barth, most of us here believe you are the greatest theologian alive. You have written dozens and dozens of books. What is the most profound idea that you have ever thought?" Barth answered without hesitation: "Jesus loves me."

That is simplicity. Aquinas, from his heavenly bleacher seat, must have smiled at that answer. Indeed, he may have inspired it.

When, on his deathbed, Thomas made his general confession, his confessor stumbled out of the room in tears, stammering: "The sins of a child of five! The sins of a child of five!"

There was a certain old teacher who said, "Unless you become as little children, you cannot enter into my Father's kingdom." There are other teachers who speak instead of an "adult Christianity" for a "mankind come of age". Please remember two things when you hear such teachers (as you certainly will). First, what "adult" means in our culture. What is an "adult" bookstore or an "adult" movie? (This is no accident—that is what they *mean* by "adult" Christianity—one with no sense of sin or guilt—and not with respect to insider trading or racism

or violence, but always only with respect to sex.) Second, remember what that old teacher said about the new teachers—
something about millstones . . .

3. Purity

Which brings us to purity. Here, as with simplicity, there is
a connection between head and heart. Moral purity produces
mental purity, as moral simplicity produces mental simplicity.
Aquinas was called the "Angelic Doctor" not only because he
knew a lot about angels but also because he was as undisturbed
by his passions as an angel, because he had a supernatural gift
of chastity. God wanted Thomas' mind to be remarkably clear,
so he healed him from the addiction that blinds us. Addictions
always blind—drunks simply cannot think clearly, whether
booze-drunks, sex-drunks, power-drunks, or money-drunks.
    The story here is well known: his family, scandalized that
Thomas would join an order of mendicant friars and shun the
worldly power and glory they had planned for him, locked him
in a tower and tossed in a prostitute to tempt him. Now there
is a natural connection between intellectual prostitution and
bodily prostitution, and Thomas knew it. His simplicity saved
his purity. With no hesitation, he grabbed a flaming brand from
the fireplace and thrust her out the door. It was, incidentally, a
good illustration of his own teaching on violence, that "a little
violence, used, can be a good thing."
    The decline of true liberal arts education in our day—the
politicizing and ideologizing of scholarship—is closely connected with sexual impurity—and Aquinas would be an excel-
lent patron to invoke against both related diseases. For "liberal
arts" means seeking truth freely, not slavishly—purely for its
own sake, not as a means or servant to some other end, to
gratify your personal desires, your agenda, or your political
correctness. A free and liberal mind is pure in its motive. It
follows the argument, not the agenda. And a free lover loves

the other as other, with charity, not cupidity. Lust, on the other hand, uses the other person's body to gratify one's own desire. Instead of willing the objective good of the other, it wills the subjective good of the self. The names of some of the prostitutes in our current intellectual whorehouse are Deconstructionism, Outcome-Based Education, Multiculturalism, and Political Correctness. Let us fight them with firebrands, as did our patron. They cannot be argued with, only exorcised.

A pure mind is like pure glass or pure water: transparent to the light. Nothing is more obvious in Aquinas' writing than this transparency. There is no mud on his mirror. His angelic intellect is like a tranquil pool, its surface unruffled by the winds of passion, so still that it reflects the stars. Once the winds blow on a pool, the stars disappear.

4. Silence

Why is silence important for anyone except monks?

The very question shows a misunderstanding. Monks are not freaks but signs, special only in showing more clearly something that is universal, an essential ingredient each life should have, only in different proportions. Monasteries are not escapes but dynamos, centers of spiritual energy, existing not for themselves but for the world. We all need monastic silence, and never more than when we have forgotten why we need it.

Kierkegaard, the greatest Protestant thinker who ever lived, almost became a Catholic (or might have become a Catholic if he had lived longer) because of his admiration for Catholic monasticism. He often wrote about silence. For example (from the *Journals*): "If I were a physician, and I could prescribe only one remedy for all the ills of the modern world, I would prescribe silence. For even if the Word of God be proclaimed in the modern world, no one can hear it; there is too much noise. Therefore, first create silence."

This means two things: interior and exterior silence. Aquinas had both. He cultivated exterior silence; he simply did not talk much. His classmates at the university called him the "Dumb Ox". It took another saint, his teacher Albert the Great, to perceive that this was the silence of a mystic, not the silence of a melonhead. He prophesied, "You may call him the Dumb Ox, but I tell you that his bellowing will one day be heard throughout the world." A very strange image for the seraphic syllogisms of the *Summa*—"bellowing"—but Albert was right, of course. A good prophet need not be a good poet.

Aquinas was not chatty. His writing does not quack like a duck. It is laconic, like the sayings of Christ and unlike the ravings of the occultists. You can usually tell a fake mystic from a true one just by counting syllables. There is not a wasted syllable anywhere in the four thousand pages of the *Summa*. His words are like bullets: hard, clear, pointed, effective, *aimed*. He would not fit in well at a fashionable Hollywood party.

Beneath the exterior silence lay an interior one. The two reinforce each other, for interior silence expresses itself in exterior silence. You can not only hear this in Gregorian chant but even see it in medieval sculpture and architecture. And the exterior silence makes the attainment of the interior silence much easier. (Ever try to meditate with the TV on?)

Hell is full of noise and is exporting this product rapidly into our world, hoping that someday no nook or cranny of the farthest island will be free of din, hoping that all islands will be colonies of Manhattan Island. For hell is the lack of love, and "if I have not love, I am a noisy gong and a clanging cymbal." In heaven, on the contrary, the three universal languages are silence, music, and love.

You can hear the silence when you read Aquinas. It is like the space in a Chinese landscape painting. It leaps out at you. It is more obvious than the sound. The words define the silence, cut the silhouette of the silence, line the outer edge of the silence. The words are powerful because they emerge from the silence like little children playing peek-a-boo or hide-and-seek. You think each word came into existence a minute before you read it. The *Summa* seems to have been written at the creation of the world.

Silence is the origin of speech, as woman is the origin of man. It is the womb of words. Our culture will never reverse what Karl Stern called its "flight from woman" until it reverses its flight from silence. Catching Thomas' mental habit can help throw us into reverse gear—which is true progress when you are headed down into the abyss.

Mary is a paragon of silence. She, too, is laconic. Her Magnificat, like Thomas' poetry, is childlike and simple: silence made palpable by words. For Mary, like Thomas, had the habit of silently "pondering all these things in her heart". Pondering is much like wondering; the difference is only one letter. And wonder, Aquinas knew, both from his philosophical authorities and from his experience, is the origin of philosophy. If philosophy means simply the love of wisdom, Mary rather than Socrates or Aristotle is the greatest philosopher. I know Thomas would accept that correction.

The themes are connected. Silence is to noise as purity to impurity, virgin to prostitute, *the* Madonna to Madonna.

5. Humility

Aquinas is humble. "Humble" comes from "humus", earth. Aquinas is earthy. He is full of common sense and examples from ordinary life—colors and animals and ships and fire and eyes and bodies and sorrows and time and movement. He moves easily between heaven and earth—he talks of God and Providence and Fate and Eternity and Angels and Universals, but also of deer and water and boats and boots and bread. He dispenses with the middleman, the pretentious and artificial midrange of sociological, psychological, and political abstractions that eat up so much of our attention and time. He connects his heaven with the humble earth as immediately in his thought as God did in his Incarnation. He sees an analogy to the circumincession of Persons in the Trinity in the biology of worms (!) and an analogy to man's ultimate aspiration, the Beatific Vision, in the fact that fire naturally moves upward and stones down.

A second meaning of humility is personal transparency, getting out of the way, like a good matchmaker. John, meet Mary —Mary, meet John. Reader, meet Truth. Reader, meet yourself. Reader, meet God. It is never: "Meet *me*." Aquinas is a window with hardly any marks on it. You do not notice the window; you notice everything else through it. Like the Holy Spirit—he testifies to Christ, not to himself. And like Christ: his words and his will are not his but the Father's. Aquinas almost disappears. If he were to meet me now, and if I were to ask him what he most wanted me to say about him, he would answer: "Talk about God, not me. Praise God, not me. 'He must increase, I must decrease.' "

As Chesterton points out, this is the secret of levitation: taking yourself lightly, almost disappearing. Angels, Chesterton says, can fly precisely because they take themselves lightly. I would not be surprised to see the great bulk of the Dumb Ox levitating just below this ceiling like a child's balloon.

A third meaning of humility is stepping back from your own achievements, comparing them, not with something less, but with something more. Having high ideals is part of humility. Having humble ideals is part of pride. Aquinas compared his *Summa*—merely the greatest theology text of all time—not to lesser texts, but to what he called the true meaning of theology as a science: the science of God and the blessed in heaven, the heavenly vision of God. When that vision was vouchsafed to him for a moment, he refused to write again and said that all he had written was only "straw". This is exactly like what Saint Paul said in Philippians when he compared all his earthly achievements to his personal knowledge of God in Christ—a Pharisee of the Pharisees, blameless as touching the law, educated by sitting at the feet of Gamaliel, "the Light of Israel", a Roman citizen—all this, compared with knowing Christ,

he called *skubala*. Look it up. Its English equivalent is also an
S-word, and the bold and literal translators of the Douay and
King James versions dared to declare the word—"dung". That
is even humbler than "straw". Very earthy indeed.

6. Detachment

Detachment is the opposite of greed. Greed is the sin Christ
warned against more than any other. (So did Buddha.) Detachment is the subject of the first Beatitude. Divine wisdom did
not place this Beatitude first by accident. (That is how God
differs from the Cross Bronx Expressway—no accidents.) The
"poverty of spirit" it declares blessed means the willingness to
be poor, whether one is poor or rich. It matters not how many
bills are filling up your wallet but how many are filling up your
soul.

There is an incident that illustrates Aquinas' detachment
from worldly riches and at the same time his attachment to un-
worldly riches. Traveling to Paris with some companions, he
came to a place where the road turned to reveal the whole city
gleaming in the sun beneath them. His companion remarked,
"How beautiful it is! Wouldn't it be grand to own everything
you can see from here?" Aquinas' dry and laconic reply was:
"I'd rather have the missing manuscript of Saint John Chrysos-
tom." First things first.

When someone has as accurate a scale of values as that, he
appears eccentric. For he is right side up in a world that is up-
side down. There is simply no proportion between the goods
of the body and the good of the mind. One idea is more valuable than a million cities. As the Book of Wisdom says (wisely,
of course), wisdom cannot be bought for any amount of gold.
(But please do not tell that to the people at Boston College
who pay my salary.)

7. Courtesy

If there are three values that have most conspicuously disappeared from our culture, they are chastity, courage, and courtesy. Few even think of courtesy as a virtue. Most think it is an artifice, or even an affectation. I would highly recommend to such people that they read that most wise and commonsensical columnist Miss Manners, who makes a very strong case for courtesy as the seedbed for all other virtues. Courtesy makes it easy to be virtuous—habitual, expected, second nature. Even if courtesy is only *playing* morality, like a stage play, even if it is only practice, rehearsal for the real thing, so to speak, still in order to practice you have actually to *practice*, actually to do it.

Plato also understood the importance of the social environment as a seedbed for morality when he insisted that young people should be exposed to beautiful and harmonious things, especially good music, because then when reason comes later to grow in them, it will have instinctively good patterns to follow. Manners are largely unconscious, but the unconscious can mightily help (or harm) the conscious. The subcontinent of the unconscious has surely been explored more in our day than in Aquinas', and I think the Freudians' mistake has not been in seeing too much in it but too little.

The incident from Aquinas' life that comes to mind concerns courtesy to an animal—all the more remarkable in light of the fact that one of Aquinas' few errors was his opinion that there were no animals in heaven. Aquinas traveled a lot across Christendom, especially between Italy and Paris, but he did not ride on a donkey, as his companions did. He walked. The obvious reason was his bulk. It was out of courtesy to the donkey that he did not impose that formidable burden on the poor innocent beast.

Aquinas' courtesy also shines through his writings, especially in his treatment of his opponents. He always states their position more perfectly and clearly and convincingly than they do before he refutes it. This is the exact opposite of the methods of modern politicians and even most modern philosophers: the making and unmaking of straw men. I think our whole world would take a gigantic step toward sanity and wisdom if it practiced only one of the rules of courtesy that ruled medieval debate, a rule Aquinas followed to a T. Before you may refute your opponent's position, you must first summarize it in your own words to his satisfaction.

And, of course, Aquinas always refutes his opponent's position, not his opponent. He is almost always impersonal rather than personal. That is because he believed so strongly in that silly old superstition of objective truth. He hardly ever resorted to name-calling. When he did, it was the idea, not the philosopher, that he insulted—as when he wrote of "the really stupid (*stultitiam*) thesis of David of Dinant's" that God and prime matter were the same since both were infinite and formless. This "really stupid thesis", by the way, is repeated by Hegel. One wonders what words Aquinas would reserve for Nietzsche's ideas or for those of Boston College professor Mary Daly, who, like Nietzsche, has idealized the Antichrist.

It is the rarity of his invective that makes it effective, like diamonds or pre-inflation money or pre-sixties sex. I once broke up a graduate class into a full sixty seconds of laughter by, first, listening politely to a ten-minute tirade of pretentious Heideggerian jargon from an arrogant Bright Young Thing, who then asked me how I would describe that idea, and then replying that I would choose the category of bullshit. Like "a little judicious violence", a little judicious uncourtesy can be very effective. But only when courtesy is normal and presupposed and expected.

8. Science

Science is not a *thing* but a habit for Aquinas. It is not in books but in souls. It is an intellectual virtue, by which we apply principles to cases, whether theoretical or practical. Aristotle and Saint Albert the Great, Aquinas' dead and living teachers,

were both very good at it. So was he. Albert, in fact, was so
good that he was suspected of wizardry.

I have found ever since the seventies that science majors
tend to make better philosophy students than humanities majors. Their minds are still structured and disciplined by the
order of nature, which reflects the order of God, while humanities majors increasingly have minds as muddled as their
models, the relativists and subjectivists who have no objective,
incorrigible data to bump up against and be disciplined by.

Theology is a science for Aquinas. It depends on principles
established by a higher science, as music depends on mathemat-
ics and surveying depends on geometry. The higher science is
the science of God; that is, the knowledge God has of us, not
the knowledge we have of God. The data of theology is divine revelation, God's word about man rather than man's word
about God. What a revolutionary idea—someone should tell
the good news to the theology departments in our Catholic
colleges. Maybe our Jesuit colleges, too.

First principles are indubitable. Only hypocrites and mad-
men pretend to doubt the Law of Non-contradiction. But science moves from principles to conclusions and is often only
probable—like a boat departing from the land: it is only probably going to float. Aquinas knew this so well that he labeled the
Ptolemaic geocentric astronomy of his time only a hypothesis
that saved the appearances, not an absolute truth, even though
it was the only hypothesis around. If he had only been around
at the time of Galileo, the whole affair could have been resolved amicably. If he were only around in our century, when
evolution is in the same position as medieval geocentric astronomy, both sides in the ongoing Scopes trial might be a bit
less shrill and dogmatic.

Dogmatism and skepticism are the ever-tempting extremes.
But both destroy philosophy, because both destroy question-
ing, wondering—philosophy's origin. Why search for truth if
truth is unattainable? Why search for truth if truth is already
attained? This brings us to Aquinas' ninth quality.

9. Curiosity

The thing that killed the cat keeps alive the philosophers. Aquinas was curious about everything (at least everything natural or supernatural, everything God was, everything he did, and everything he made). This is so obvious from his commodious work that it is virtually impossible to pick out one special passage. His mind is evidently like a vacuum cleaner eagerly sucking in every speck of dust.

This curiosity came out very early in his life. The story has it that at the age of four he asked his mother the stunningly simple question "What is God?" And since his mother's answer evidently did not satisfy him, he set about writing the *Summa Theologiae.*

10. Wholeness

The tenth and perhaps most precious gift Aquinas' life and work can offer us is his wholeness. In the memorable formula of Gilson, "he made it possible for our thought to be one with our prayer." As our next speaker will no doubt demonstrate, Aquinas' marriage of Faith and Reason was one of the happiest marriages we have ever seen. The two became one flesh, one body, without ceasing to be two, as a man becomes, not less masculine, but more so when he marries a woman, and a woman becomes more feminine, not less, by marrying a man. Faith is the mother of sanctity, and reason is the father of philosophy, and the children of this marriage of faith and reason— philosophy and sanctity—are also married in Aquinas' life and work.

Philosophy and sanctity do not seem to many people to be a couple who are obvious candidates for marriage. Yet I know few books more suitable for meditation than the *Summa* and few human prayers more perfect to offer to God than that whole immense cathedral of thought.

Perhaps Thomas' supreme triumph, however, is not the *Summa* at all but the liturgy he composed for the Feast of Corpus Christi. For one thing, that is more truly a cathedral, for a medieval cathedral was essentially a penumbra for the Eucharist, a glorious robe for the broken Body of Christ, a dining room fittingly ornate to contain the cup of his Blood. In the words of this liturgy, we perceive a perfect unity of the three deepest human ideals—the true, the good, and the beautiful. It is philosophically perfect, prayerfully pious, and poetically pulchritudinous. Contemplating it makes you simultaneously wise, holy, and delighted. A foretaste of heaven. What more can anyone give us on earth: an appetizer for the meal we will eat eternally at the heavenly banquet fed not by Aquinas but directly by the hand of his Lord—and ours.

Marie I. George

"TRUST ME." "WHY SHOULD I?" AQUINAS ON FAITH AND REASON

I. Introduction

What has Athens to do with Jerusalem? So asked Tertullian in the second century (A.D.). People nowadays, laboring under misconceptions of freedom and rationality, are more likely to ask the opposite question: What has Jerusalem to do with Athens? Much is at stake in answering the many questions that arise concerning the relation of faith and reason. It is hard to say which has more grave consequences: to cast off reason as a whore, as Luther would have it, or to reject tenets of the faith because they seem to fly in the face of reason. It is hard to say which is the sorrier state of affairs: the Christian who can give no explanation of his beliefs[1] or the one who understands what is proposed but who thinks that the beliefs need to be updated or "reinterpreted", meaning explained away.

According to Leo XIII, the faithful would be preserved from these serious errors concerning the relation of faith and reason if they would turn to the teachings of the Angelic Doctor:

> [We] remind each and all of you that our first and most cherished idea is that you should all furnish . . . to studious youth . . . [the] wisdom flowing . . . from the Angelic Doctor. Many are the reasons why we are so desirous of this. . . . Many of those who, with minds alienated from the faith, hate Catholic institutions, claim reason as their sole mistress and guide. Now, we think that, apart from the supernatural help of God, noth-

ing is better calculated to heal those minds . . . than the solid doctrine of the Fathers and the scholastics, who so clearly and forcibly demonstrate the firm foundation of the faith, its divine origin, its certain truth . . . and its perfect accord with reason, in a manner to satisfy completely minds open to persuasion, however unwilling and repugnant.[2]

Aquinas composed no treatise entitled "Faith and Reason". However, he addresses questions concerning the two in the numerous places where he treats of faith. The relation between them is of particular concern to him in the *Summa Contra Gentiles*, for the purpose of this work is to explain and defend the faith before a Muslim audience. Lacking as common ground the same sacred writings, Aquinas turns to what can be naturally known by human reason. Whence the preface of the *Summa Contra Gentiles* discusses what reason can and cannot show in regard to matters of faith. It served as my starting point for the following sketch of Aquinas' thought on some of the more fundamental questions concerning faith and reason.

When Saint Thomas addresses questions of faith and reason, he commonly talks first about faith or belief in general, since this is more readily understood. Then he goes on to consider what is specific to supernatural faith. What he says about belief or faith in general is the following: Faith is a kind of intellectual knowledge in the broad sense of knowledge—one has to apprehend by reason the truths that one is believing. One could not believe that a woman bore a child unless one understood in some way what a woman is and what bearing children is. Insofar as faith requires reason, it is plainly not opposed to reason. Opposition between the two lies rather in that reason when knowing adheres to truths because of being convinced by evidence, whereas reason when believing adheres to truths without adequate evidence but rather because it is commanded by the will to do so. This is what distinguishes the act of knowing, taking knowing in the strict sense, from the act of believing: To know depends on having evidence for something, or having a logical proof that is based on evidence. To believe is to accept something unseen as true on the word of another.[3] Thus, one cannot know and believe the same thing in the same respect:[4] one cannot believe that it is snowing outside if one sees it. One cannot believe that the angles of a triangle equal two right angles if one has proven it.[5]

Note that we understand what the activity of "believing" is more readily than what faith is (namely, the habit or habitual disposition of the soul to believe); the latter is only known through the former. For the sake of clarity and brevity, I will thus more often refer to the activity than the habit. Note also that Aquinas uses the expression "natural reason" when he is talking about reason knowing things in virtue of its own natural capacity rather than in the light of faith.

One might wonder whether faith does not involve a misuse of reason: Is one not acting irrationally if one holds to something, not on the basis of evidence, but because of an act of the will—for example, a couch potato might choose to believe the Plompette Sofa Company's study that shows that moderate exercise is deleterious to one's health; or little brother might choose to believe that Martians live in the outhouse because big sister says so. However, it is not always unreasonable to adhere to something on the word of another. To the contrary, as Aquinas points out, when it comes to the business of everyday life, no one can suffice for themselves, and so we are obliged to trust others.[6] We trust that our food is not contaminated, that schedules are accurate, that when we have a green light, the light the other way is red. As Aquinas points out, if we were to doubt everything that others told us, we would have to doubt who our father was (that was before the days of genetic testing).[7] We are clearly better off for believing people. However, in order to have reasonable belief, we must not believe just anyone indiscriminately; we should use reason to discern which people are trustworthy and which are not. In the case of reasonable belief, then, the will moves reason to adhere to certain things as true because some good will be achieved by doing so, and reason guides this motion of the will insofar as it establishes what the good is and that the one believed is worthy of belief.

Once again, even reasonable faith is contrary to reason in the sense that it is contrary to the intellect's proper mode of operation, which is to adhere to things in light of evidence. In Aquinas' words,

> [T]he intellect of the believer is said to be [held] captive, because it is governed according to foreign terms, and not according to its own. . . . Whence it is that in the one who believes there may even rise up a motion regarding the contrary of what he most firmly holds, although this does not happen in the one understanding or knowing with certitude.[8]

Faith, both natural and supernatural, holds the intellect captive. The intellect naturally desires to see for itself. The intellect's bondage under supernatural faith is meant to pass away once faith has guided us to our heavenly home: "Simply speaking, the ultimate end of the faith itself, that which we intend [to obtain] from faith, is beatitude in heaven (*in patria*) which consists in a clear vision of God."[9]

Let us turn now from a consideration of faith taken generally to Aquinas' definition of supernatural faith. This definition specifies the content of belief and the one whom we believe: "Believing is an act of the intellect assenting to divine truth by command of the will moved by God through grace."[10] A better understanding of this definition can be arrived at by addressing the following questions regarding faith and reason: Why is it reasonable for the intellect to be moved by the will as to faith in God? That is, what are the goods to be attained that warrant making an act of faith? And how do we know that the one whom we believe is trustworthy? Finally one might ask: How does the content of the faith, the truths proposed for belief, compare with what is known through reason?

As to the first question, Aquinas, in his commentary on the Creed, names four goods that belief in God obtains.[11] The first of these is that "through faith the soul is joined to God: for through faith the Christian soul enters into a certain marriage, as it were, with God. 'Without faith, it is impossible to please God' (Heb 11:6)." The intimate union of God and the soul through faith is also spoken of thus by Aquinas: "[A]s the body lives with natural life through the soul, so the soul lives the life of grace through God. God, however, first inhabits the soul through faith. 'Christ lives through faith in your hearts' (Eph 3:17)."[12]

The second good faith accomplishes is that it causes eternal life to begin in us: "This is eternal life to know the one true God, and the one he sent, Jesus Christ" (Jn 17:3).[13] Faith allows us to know God, albeit "through a glass darkly".[14] For this reason Saint Paul says that faith is "the substance of things hoped for",[15] "substance" meaning the foundation upon which the hope is based, and "the things hoped for" being the Beatific Vision[16] and the things attendant upon it, "the bodily perfections and the society of the saints".[17]

Thirdly, faith teaches us to live well while we are on earth. "For it teaches us that there is one God, who is rewarder of the good and punisher of the bad; and that there is another life . . . by which we are sufficiently drawn to the good, and so that we might avoid evil."[18]

Aquinas sums up the second and third goods in a striking way: "None of the philosophers before the coming of Christ [even] with their entire effort were able to know so much about God and about the things necessary for eternal life as after the coming of Christ one little old lady knows through faith."[19]

Finally, faith benefits us by helping us to avoid the temptations of the world, the flesh, and the devil by clearly teaching us to whom we owe obedience and about goods everlasting.

The Christian faith thus offers the greatest possible good: " '[W]ithout faith it is impossible to please God', when it is taken away, nothing remains in a man profitable for his eternal salvation, on which account it is written that 'an apostate is good for nothing.' "[20] The words we believe are "the words of eternal life" (Jn 6:70); words of eternal life, both because they indicate the way to eternal life and because they are a foretaste of the knowledge of God which is eternal life.[21]

Our next question is whether faith is reasonable from the point of view of the reliability of the person whom we believe. Here the answer is initially very simple: It is none other than God himself,[22] who can neither deceive nor be deceived.[23]

How, though, do we know that we are believing God? Saint Thomas says:

> One who believes does have a sufficient motive for believing, namely, the authority of God's teaching, confirmed by miracles, and—what is greater—the inner inspiration of God inviting him to believe.[24]

We are disposed to believe people for two sorts of reasons. One is on the basis of external signs of their reliability: for example, because their testimony accords with known facts and/or with the testimony of others whom we believe to be reliable. The second way we can be disposed to believing someone is due to our personal contact with them, by which we have become assured that we can trust them. Now God both offers us external indications that the truths of the faith come from him and extends a personal invitation to us.

Before examining the external signs that establish that the Catholic Church genuinely speaks in God's name, let us note that a certain naturally acquirable knowledge about God can dispose people to faith in God.[25] For believing someone presupposes that one knows: first, that the person exists; second, that the person is good and thus will not deceive one; and, finally, that the person is more knowledgeable[26] about the matter to be believed than oneself. Aquinas maintains that by natural reason one can come to know with certitude that God exists and that he is all-good and all-wise.[27] This knowledge renders the event of God's speaking to man credible. Of course the person who has arrived at such knowledge, while being open to the possibility of revelation in virtue of that knowledge, still only knows *about* God rather than knowing God personally.

How, though, is one to know that God has in fact spoken? We cannot believe the good news unless we have heard it, and we cannot hear it unless someone announces it to us.[28] A problem arises because by use of our senses we do not perceive God to speak to us. Rather we hear what God has revealed when it is announced to us by other human beings. How can we know that a given preacher speaks in God's name? How do we know that it is those who preach in conformity with the doctrine of the Catholic Church who genuinely speak in God's name? The authenticity of the Church is not something that can be proven to be necessarily the case; rather, it is indicated by signs,[29] such as miracles[30] and the quasi-miraculous spread of Christianity.[31] These signs are of sufficient weight to render belief in the Church reasonable, and unbelief unreasonable. However, they are not of such weight that they necessarily convince those who see them; one remains free to believe or not. In order for these signs to convince someone, God's grace is necessary. As Aquinas explains:

> As to assent to matters of faith, we can look to two types of cause. One is a cause that persuades from without, e.g., a miracle witnessed or a human appeal urging belief. No such cause is enough, however; one man believes and another does not, when both have seen the same miracle, heard the same preaching. Another kind of cause must therefore be present, an inner cause, one that influences a person inwardly to assent to the things of faith. . . . [S]ince in assenting to the things of faith a person is raised above his own nature, he has this assent from a supernatural source influencing him; this source is God. The assent of faith, which is its principal act, therefore, has as its cause God, moving us inwardly through grace.[32]

Without the internal invitation of God, no one could believe. Faith is a gift offered to us by God,[33] who speaks to us within;[34] it is not something that man can acquire through

his own efforts. It is, however, by an act of free will that we
accept or reject this gift. Aquinas often cites Saint Augustine,
who says "no one believes unless he is willing."[35] If we had
no free choice in regard to the faith, our act of faith could
not be meritorious.[36] Aquinas thus holds that "[b]elief is . . .
a matter of the believer's will, but a person's will needs to be
prepared by God through his grace in order to be lifted up to
what surpasses nature."[37]

The relation between the external evidence for the faith and
the internal inspiration from God explains why Aquinas, on
the one hand, maintains that the reasonable person asks for
signs to substantiate the credibility of the one believed[38] and
yet, at the same time, tells us that those whom God has invited
interiorly should not demand signs as a condition for believing.
There is a readiness to believe that amounts to gullibility, and
there is a readiness to believe that is due to goodness. Christ
himself says: "It is an evil and adulterous generation that asks
for a sign" (Mt 12:39); and "Blessed are those who do not ˙
see and yet believe" (Jn 20:29). The disbelief of the Pharisees
who had seen Christ raise Lazarus from the dead plainly did
not stem from any rational doubt. As Aquinas notes:

> [The Pharisees] were saying "what should we do, because this
> man works many signs?" . . . They were not less stupid than
> blind: for they were doubting what they ought to do when
> there was nothing else for them to do than believe. The matter
> of doubt, however, was because they were afraid that harm might
> befall them . . . first, the loss of their spiritual leadership. . . .
> Second, . . . of temporal possessions.[39]

The skeptical Nathanael, on the other hand, is praised by
Christ for being without guile. As Aquinas points out, Nathanael reasonably questions Philip's claim that Jesus of Nazareth
is the Messiah, for the Scriptures do not clearly indicate that
the savior is to come from Nazareth. Philip, however, presses
Nathanael to come and see Christ for himself, assuring him that
then his doubts will be laid to rest. And, indeed, when Christ

reveals to Nathanael what would have been hidden to a mere mortal, Nathanael, being of good will, immediately believes in him.[40] For "granted that to believe men quickly pertains to thoughtlessness (*levitas*) . . . , nevertheless, to believe God quickly is, to the contrary, praiseworthy."[41]

Belief in God brings us the most certain kind of knowledge we can have:

> Whence in the faith by which we believe in God, not only is there an accepting of the thing to which we assent, but something which inclines to assent; and this is a certain light which is the habit of faith that is divinely infused in the human mind: which certainly is more sufficient to inducing [assent] than some demonstration, [for] even if demonstration may never conclude what is false, nevertheless in regard to it man frequently errs in that what he thinks to be a demonstration is not one. Faith is even more sufficient than the natural light itself by which we assent to principles; since that light is frequently impeded by bodily infirmity as happens in the mentally ill. The light of faith, however, which is as a certain seal of the first truth in the mind, is not able to be mistaken, as God is neither able to deceive or lie. Whence this light suffices for judging. This habit nevertheless does not move by way of the intellect, but rather by way of the will: whence it does not cause one to see the things which are believed; nor does it compel assent, but causes one to assent voluntarily. And thus it is manifest that faith comes from two things; from God, namely, as to the interior light which induces assent: and from those who propose things exteriorly, which things take their beginning from divine revelation. . . . [S]o faith is from hearing (*ex auditu*), and nevertheless the habit of faith is infused.[42]

God, as the one whom we believe, is what Aquinas calls the formal object of the faith, that is, we believe the truths of the faith under the formality "revealed by God", just as a child believes certain things "because Mommy or Daddy said so". Faith first of all is faith in someone. This is why Aquinas says that, if a person rejects one single article of the faith knowing it to be proposed as an article of faith, he does not really

have the faith. One either believes God or one does not. A
person who rejects a single thing proposed by God through
the Church may believe many other things that pertain to the
faith but does not believe them as revealed by God, but rather
because it happens for one reason or another to fit with what
that person judges to be acceptable teachings.[43]

As to the material object of the faith, the truths which we
believe, these concern God principally, along with other things
the knowledge of which helps us arrive at the vision of God.[44]
Among these beliefs, some are more central than others insofar
as they contain the others implicitly:

> [O]n the basis of Hebrews, "He that cometh to God must be-
> lieve that he is and is a rewarder to them that seek him", all
> the articles of faith are implicit in certain primary ones, namely
> that God exists and that he has providence over man's salvation.
> For the truth that God is includes everything that we believe
> to exist eternally in God and that will comprise our beatitude.
> Faith in God's providence comprises all those things that God
> arranges in history for man's salvation and that make up our
> way towards beatitude.[45]

The material object of the faith, or the content of the
faith, taking faith in the strict sense, consists of those things
about God and his providence for man that could not be
known through natural reason. Those things that can be known
through natural reason, granted that not all will arrive at such
knowledge, pertain to the faith only in a qualified way.

> Those things that exceed all human understanding cannot be
> proved through demonstration, because demonstration is found-
> ed on the understanding of principles; and therefore these things
> cannot be known (scita). But there are certain things that pre-
> cede the faith, of which there is not faith except accidentally,
> namely, insofar as they exceed the understanding of this man to
> be able to be demonstrated and known, and not of man simply
> speaking, such as that God exists: which certainly is believed by
> the person whose understanding does not arrive at the demon-
> stration. . . .[46]

The truths of the faith in the strict sense are beyond reason. However, while there is no way that reason through its natural operation could know these truths, this does not mean that they are contrary to reason. As Aquinas explains:

> [W]hat is divinely said through apostles and prophets is never contrary to those things that natural reason dictates. Nevertheless something that is said exceeds the comprehension of reason; and seems to be very much contrary to reason, although it is not contrary—as to a simple person it seems contrary to reason that the sun is greater than the earth, since it is the size of a dime—which to the wise, nevertheless, appears reasonable.[47]

Thus far we have explained the definition of supernatural faith and have shown that divine faith is reasonable both in respect to the goods obtained by believing and in respect to the reliability of the one whom we believe. We have also addressed what is meant by saying that the content of the faith is beyond reason. Now we will go on to consider whether it is profitable or detrimental to use natural reason in matters of faith.

II. Ways in Which the Use of Natural Reason Is Beneficial to Faith:

Aquinas says that there are three ways in which reason can be of use in regard to matters of faith: First, it can demonstrate preambles of the faith; second, it can help one attain a deeper understanding of the faith; and, finally, it allows one to defend the faith.[48] Let us consider each of these ways one by one.

Reason is beneficial to faith to the extent that it is able to establish the preambles, the chief of which would be the existence of God, and then his attributes (omnipotence, omniscience, providence, and so on). As Aquinas points out:

> that God is one according as this is demonstrated is not said to be an article of faith but is presupposed to the articles of faith:

for the knowledge of faith presupposes natural knowledge, as grace [presupposes] nature.[49]

Unlike the articles of faith in the strict sense, which cannot be known by natural reason, the preambles that bear on God's existence and attributes can be,[50] and ideally (in an adult) would be, demonstratively known prior to faith. In accord with what Saint Paul says, Aquinas holds that the human mind is naturally constituted to know certain truths about God. In many places he cites Romans 1:20: "Ever since God created the world his everlasting power and deity—however invisible—have been there for the mind to see in the things he has made." Aquinas regards those who do not make use of natural reason to investigate the preambles to be worthy of blame.[51]

God does, however, also reveal the preambles, and they are an object of faith for most. For few there are who actually arrive at demonstrative knowledge of the preambles, and it takes them a long time to do so. For this reason, as Aquinas points out in many places, God in his goodness reveals the preambles so that the people who would not eventually come to know them by natural reason would be able to know them and so that those who would eventually arrive at such knowledge would not be left in the dark before they did so.[52]

Aquinas raises the question of whether those who come to know the preambles through natural reason having previously held them by faith lose the merit of faith, and he responds that while this knowledge subtracts belief, it does not diminish the merit that is due to charity, on the condition that the person's motive in seeking to know them does not arise out of an unwillingness to believe:[53]

> For when anyone has a ready will to believe, he loves the truth he believes, he dwells upon it and treasures any supportive arguments he may discover. Then human reasoning does not take away the merit of faith, but is rather a sign of a greater merit.[54]

A second way that reason can be useful is for coming to a deeper understanding of the truths of the faith, taking faith in the strict sense.[55] Aquinas avoids two extreme positions: one that claims that natural reason is but little less adequate to dealing with sacred mysteries than it is to grappling with the difficult truths of metaphysics; while the other extreme maintains that reason is entirely useless here.

That Aquinas rejects the former is clear from what was said earlier: an understanding of the truths of the faith, unlike an understanding of the truths of metaphysics, is beyond even the best philosophers' capacities:

> The truths about God thus far proposed [that God is one, simple, perfect, infinite, intelligent, and endowed with will] have been subtly discussed by a number of pagan philosophers, although some of them erred concerning these matters. And those who propounded true doctrine in this respect were scarcely able to arrive at such truths even after long and painstaking investigation. But there are other truths about God revealed to us in the teaching of the Christian religion, which were beyond the reach of the philosophers. These are truths about which we are instructed, in accord with the norm of Christian faith, in a way that transcends human perception.[56]

The philosopher who has the vigor of mind to have traveled the long road that begins in sense experience to arrive at some understanding of the first immaterial cause of being upon entering the realm of faith suddenly finds himself completely inadequate. Theology is not just natural theology or metaphysics taken one step farther. Christ says: "I bless you, Father, . . . for hiding these things from the learned and the clever and revealing them to mere children. . . . [N]o one knows . . . who the Father is except the Son and those to whom the Son chooses to reveal him" (Lk 10:22).

Consider, for example, human knowledge about divine providence. There were pagan philosophers who understood that it is responsible for the order of the universe. However, there are many things that pertain to God's providence that they never could have known.[57] Indeed, if they were told that certain things were to come about by providence, their initial reaction would be to reject the suggestions as absurd. Here of course we are referring to the mystery of the Incarnation and to the Cross of Jesus Christ.[58]

> [T]he announcement of the Cross of Christ . . . seems to be something foolish . . . that is, to nonbelievers who estimate themselves wise according to the world's standards, because the declaration of the Cross of Christ contains something that according to human wisdom seems to be impossible, namely, that God would die, that the omnipotent one would be subjected to violence at [man's] hands. It even contains something which seems to be contrary to the prudence of this world, namely, that someone would not flee being confounded when he could.[59]

Once such mysteries have been revealed to us, however, it is appropriate for us to use reason to try to understand them more deeply.[60] Though human reason is inadequate to proving the truths of the faith, nonetheless it can offer arguments of fittingness and comparisons that can help us better understand them. Aquinas' treatment of the Incarnation and the Passion are illustrative of this. He opens both discussions by pointing out that God is able to do all things, and thus if he has done something one way, it is not because he was unable to accomplish it some other way, but rather because it was more fittingly done that way. Consequently, while one could not prove that God had to become man and die on the Cross, the person who knows through revelation that this has happened can investigate reasons for why it is fitting that God has done so. Aquinas, after giving numerous reasons for the appropriateness of the Incarnation, closes with the words: "There were many other advantages resulting [from the Incarnation], which are beyond our present earth-bound comprehension",[61] thereby warning us that it would be pretentious to think that one's investigation of the mysteries of the faith could ever be complete.

Aquinas calls the reasonings used to deepen an understanding of the faith "weak" in the sense that such arguments are never demonstrative; for example, one cannot prove that God is Triune. Whence Aquinas warns us that they are not to be used for purposes of convincing adversaries of the truth of the faith, for "the very inadequacy of the arguments would rather strengthen them in their error, since they would imagine that our acceptance of the truth of faith was based on such weak arguments."[62] Nonetheless, such arguments bring the greatest solace and delight to the believer who has no presumptions as to comprehending the faith fully.[63]

Even learning drawn from secular authors, be they poets, orators, philosophers, or others, is to be drawn upon to the extent that it is useful for deepening one's understanding of the truths of the faith. As Aquinas observes:

> The Apostle, Titus 1:12, uses the verse of Epimenidis the poet . . . , and 1 Corinthians 12:33, the words of Menander . . . and in the Acts 17:28, the words of Aratus: "Of him (namely, God) we are the people." Therefore it is also licit for other doctors of divine Scripture to use arguments of secular authors (*physicis*).[64]

Aquinas thus steers a middle course between denying any value to human reasoning in regard to matters of the faith and assigning human arguments a central role in understanding the faith.[65] For Saint Thomas, philosophy in regard to theology was a maidservant, no more, and also no less:

> Holy teaching can borrow from the other sciences, not from any need to beg from them, but for the greater clarification of the things it conveys. For it takes its principles directly from God through revelation, not from the other sciences. On that account it does not rely on them as though they were in control, for their rôle is subsidiary and ancillary; so an architect makes use of tradesmen as a statesman employs soldiers. That it turns to them so is not from any lack or insufficiency within itself, but because our understanding is wanting, which is the more readily guided into the world above reason, set forth in holy teaching, through the world of natural reason from which the other sciences take their course.[66]

A third way in which reason can be put to use in service of the faith is "to resist things which are said against the faith;

either by showing that they are false or by showing that they
are not necessary."[67] Since truth cannot contradict truth, any
argument that maintains something contrary to the faith must
always contain some error, either as to principle or as to logic.
Being versed in philosophy helps one to discern what the de-
ficiency is and thus helps one to defend the faith.[68]

Since that human reason can serve the faith in the above
three ways, one might wonder why Saint Paul often rebukes
people for having recourse to it. As Aquinas explains, there
are four ways in which people merit reprimand for using human reason to the detriment of faith: One would be if they
were to presume to comprehend perfectly the matters of faith;
another, if they were investigating matters beyond their individual capacity;[69] a third way would be if they were to make
use of "things that are contrary to the faith that do not belong to philosophy but rather to the abuse of philosophy or
to error". And finally, they could err in their use of reason
by making faith subject to the ends of philosophy, as when
"someone wants to believe nothing except what could be had
through philosophy; when, to the contrary, philosophy is to
be reduced to the ends of faith."[70]

III. How Faith Helps Natural Reason
in Its Pursuit of Truth

We have seen the uses of reason that are of service to the faith
and those that are detrimental to it. Let us now consider the
assistance faith offers to natural reason in its pursuit of truth.
The help faith offers to reason lies principally in preserving it
from error. For as mentioned above, among the things that faith
teaches us about, some are capable of being proven through
natural reason.[71] The overlap comes principally in regard to
two sorts of truth: the truths of moral philosophy and the
highest truths treated by speculative philosophy, namely, those
about the divine nature and the human soul. As for science,[72]

the faith says relatively little, for detailed knowledge about material reality helps us little in knowing God and our way to him:

> [I]n the teaching of philosophy, which considers creatures in themselves and leads us from them to the knowledge of God, the first consideration is about creatures; the last, of God. But in the teaching of faith, which considers creatures only in their relation to God, the consideration of God comes first, that of creatures afterwards. And thus the doctrine of faith is more perfect, as being more like the knowledge possessed by God, who, in knowing himself, immediately knows other things.[73]

When Scripture says something that is contrary to what is known scientifically, it is not to be criticized, for it does not intend to teach science but to start from what uneducated people take to be the case about nature, in order to lead them to understand something about things supernatural. In the words of Aquinas:

> [A]ccording to Aristotle, the stars are fixed in their spheres and actually move only with the movement of the spheres. The senses, however, perceive only the movement of the celestial bodies, not that of the spheres. And Moses, having care for the ordinary people, as we have already observed, follows what appears to the senses.[74]

To return to our main point: In regard to truths about immaterial and divine things and about morality, the great advantage that faith affords the believer is freedom from error. On these matters, the Catholic philosopher has the answer book, so to speak. When the Catholic philosopher arrives at some conclusion contrary to that of the faith, he is sure that he has made some mistake in his reasoning or in his starting points. Truth cannot contradict truth, that is, truth that we arrive at by right usage of the God-given faculty of reason cannot contradict what God directly reveals to us. As Aquinas explains:

> [T]hat which is introduced into the soul of the student by the teacher is contained in the knowledge of the teacher—unless

his teaching is fictitious, which it is improper to say of God. Now, the knowledge of the principles that are known to us naturally has been implanted in us by God; for God is the Author of our nature. These principles, therefore, are also contained by the divine Wisdom. Hence, whatever is opposed to them is opposed to the divine Wisdom, and, therefore, cannot come from God. That which we hold by faith as divinely revealed, therefore, cannot be contrary to our natural knowledge.[75]

Knowing the correct answers in advance is, of course, not a substitute for knowing them through a logical argument based on experience. Unfortunately, having the answers can lead to intellectual laziness. Catholic thinkers must fight the temptation to be satisfied with shoddy arguments when the conclusions of these arguments happen to coincide with what is known with certitude through faith. Indeed, Christian philosophers should rather be doubly careful about their reasoning, for if they offer feeble philosophical arguments in defense of something they know to be true through faith, when a keener thinker comes along and demolishes those arguments, it tends to discredit the truth of the faith.

The great advantage that faith affords the philosopher is better appreciated when one realizes that faith offers guidance principally in those areas both about which we are most desirous of knowledge and about which we are most likely to fall into error. In the speculative order, the things we most desire knowledge of are things immaterial and divine. Our minds have the greatest difficulty knowing these things, because they are non-sensible, and our minds acquire knowledge starting from sense experience.

In the practical order, the things we most seek knowledge of concern the moral life. In the moral order, it is hard to know the truth for a number of reasons: first, because the principles on which the science of ethics is based are only evident to those who have been well raised. But given the influence of original sin and actual sin, even the best of pagan societies approve of certain immoral practices; for example, Aristotle approved of exposing children under certain circumstances.[76] Secondly, the object that ethics deals with is highly variable, and thus it is hard to sort out which moral norms are absolutely true and which are true only for the most part. Thirdly, there is a problem knowing what the end of human life is, and this is especially troublesome since this knowledge constitutes the starting point for moral philosophy. As to the latter, Aquinas has the following to say:

> [I]t is necessary to anyone who is heading for happiness to know in what things he ought to seek happiness, and how: which certainly cannot come about more easily than through faith; since the inquiry of reason is not able to arrive at such things, unless many things are known in advance, which things are not easy to know. Nor even can this come about with less danger, since the inquiry of human reason easily errs because of the imbecility of our intellect: and this even is plainly shown from the philosophers themselves, who, seeking through the way of reason the end of human life and the mode of arriving at it, [and] not discovering it, fell into numerous and most base errors and were disagreeing with one another to such an extent that in regard to everything concerning these matters there is scarcely one opinion common to two or three of them: while nevertheless through faith we see even many peoples agree in one opinion.[77]

Certain Catholic thinkers go too far, however, and deny that one could have a science of ethics without reason being enlightened by faith. Aquinas in the passage above does not say that moral truths are impossible to know but that they depend on knowing many things that are difficult to know, and thus most human beings who try to reason about such matters fall into very serious errors. Certainly, the mistake of thinking that one cannot have genuine knowledge about moral action unless one has the faith is much closer to the truth than to say that there is a purely human science of ethics about which the faith has nothing to say. For the dictates of right reason concerning many matters, for example, divorce[78] and contraception,

have become obscured in the minds of men in many times
and places. Still, just as reason is naturally endowed to judge
speculative matters, so, too, is it endowed to judge practical
matters:

> [S]ince human conduct is such by its relation to reason, whatever
> conforms with reason is called good, and whatever is in disac-
> cord with reason is called bad. And just as every judgment of
> reason in the speculative order springs from the natural knowl-
> edge of first principles, so does every judgment of reason in the
> practical order spring from certain naturally known principles.[79]

> The commandments of the Decalogue are those things that nat-
> ural reason dictates; and therefore anyone whosoever is held to
> know them explicitly, nor does a like reason apply to the articles
> of the faith, which are above reason.[80]

The principles in the moral order that are evident to reason
provide the foundation for moral philosophy. Unlike certain
modern authors, Saint Thomas maintains that pagan authors,
availing themselves of human reason alone, arrived at valid
moral (and political) philosophy.[81] In response to the objec-
tion that pagan moral science is not truly science, since all
practical sciences take the end as starting point for reasoning,
and human reason unenlightened by faith is unaware of our
true end, Aquinas would point out that:

> The ultimate good of man that first moves the will as ultimate
> end is twofold. One of which is [a good] proportioned to hu-
> man nature, since for its attainment natural powers suffice; and
> this is the happiness that the philosophers spoke about. . . . The
> other good of man exceeds the proportions of human nature,
> since for its obtainment natural powers do not suffice, neither
> for thinking about [it] nor for desiring [it]; but it is promised
> to man from divine liberality alone.[82]

Albeit moral philosophy is imperfect, since it does not direct
us to our ultimate happiness, which is above nature to know
and also to achieve, this knowledge is nonetheless not opposed
to the knowledge had through faith.[83] Contrary to what cer-

tain Catholic thinkers have maintained, those who follow the
lead of natural reason are not giving a false direction to their
lives. Aquinas maintains, rather, that "if we do what we can,
namely, follow the lead of natural reason, God will not fail
us in what is necessary to us."[84] This is borne out by the
conversions of morally upright individuals such as Nathanael,
Cornelius,[85] and the centurion whose servant Christ heals.[86]
Aquinas deemed it a worthwhile endeavor to comment on the
whole of the pagan Aristotle's *Nicomachean Ethics* and upon part
of his *Politics*. His frequent references to Aristotle in the parts
of the *Summa* devoted to moral matters further confirms the
value he places on careful investigation of such questions in
light of natural reason. Again, he sees grace as building upon
nature; thus in seeking to perfect nature by natural means, we
pave the way for grace:

> [T]he gifts of grace are added to nature in such a manner that
> they do not destroy it, but rather perfect it; whence even the
> light of faith, which is instilled in us by grace, does not destroy
> the light of the natural knowledge [which light is] naturally in-
> stilled in us.[87]

The Catholic philosopher who sets aside investigating ethics
in a philosophical manner, figuring that, after all, the faith
teaches us how to live, and, indeed, more perfectly than human ethics can, forgoes, first, the benefit of being able to reason
about moral matters with other non-believing members of the
civil society in which he lives and, secondly, that of being able
to attain a more profound understanding of moral theology.
It is a sad thing when a Catholic philosopher's inability to use
natural reason to defend morality results in his views on morality being dismissed as merely personal religious beliefs. The
Christian philosopher who approaches ethics from everyday
experience of moral action will lead nonbelievers toward the
faith, since what reason rightly shows to be appropriate means
for achieving happiness necessarily coincides with the moral
teachings of the Catholic faith.[88]

Faith, then, offers reason inestimable help by providing an infallible measure of truth in regard to the truths that reason most desires to know and that reason has the greatest difficulty in knowing. This measure, while remaining one that is extrinsic to philosophy (for, again, philosophy's proper measure is the first principles known through the natural light of reason),[89] rather than being restrictive of freedom, academic or other, frees us from error. Let us close with Aquinas' commentary on the words of Christ: "Know ye the truth, and the truth will set you free":

> [C]ertainly it is a privilege of great dignity to be a disciple of Christ. . . . But a greater [privilege] yet is to know the truth, since this is the goal of the disciple. And this even the Lord gives to believers; whence he says "Know ye the truth", namely, the doctrine, which I teach you. But greatest is the acquisition of liberty, which the knowledge of the truth brings about in the believer; whence he says "And the truth will set you free." To be free, however, in this passage, does not imply exemption from any difficulty whatsoever [*angustia*] . . . but, properly speaking, to be set free. And this from three things: for the truth of doctrine will free us from the error of falsehood . . . the truth of grace will free us from the servitude of sin . . . the eternal truth, in Jesus Christ, will free us from corruption.[90]

NOTES

[1] Cf. 1 Pet 3:15.

[2] Leo XIII, *Aeterni Patris* (Boston: Daughters of St. Paul, 1979), pp. 18, 19.

[3] Cf. *Summa Contra Gentiles, On the Truth of the Catholic Faith*, trans. Vernon J. Bourke (New York: Doubleday, 1955–1957), III, 40. Hereafter cited as *SCG*.

[4] In some places he says that one cannot believe and know the same things in the *same mode*: *Summa Theologiae*, ed. Instituti Studiorum Medievalium Ottaviensis (Ottawa: Commissio Piana, 1953), II–II, 2, 3 ad 3: "With regard to the hidden things of God faith perceives them in a higher way on many points than does natural intelligence reasoning from creatures to God." Hereafter cited as *ST*.

[5] Cf. *ST* II–II, 1, 4; *ST* II–II, 1, 5; and *ST* II–II, 1, 5 ad 4.

[6] Cf. *In Librum Boethii de Trinitate*, ed. Decker (Leiden: E. J. Brill, 1959), 3, 1. Hereafter cited as *In Boe.*

[7] *In Symbolum Apostolorum, scilicet, 'Credo in Deum' Expositio* (Rome: Marietti), no. 866. Hereafter cited as *Credo*.

[8] *Quaestiones Disputatae de Veritate*, in *Quaestiones Disputatae*, vol. 1, ed. Raymundi M. Spiazzi, O.P. (Turin: Marietti, 1964), 14, 1. [Translations of this work are by the author.] Hereafter cited as *QDV*.

[9] In *Super Epistolas S. Pauli*, ed. Raphaelis Cai, O.P. (Rome: Marietti, 1953), vol. 2, Hebrews, no. 553. Hereafter cited as *Super Hebr.*

[10] *ST* II–II, 2, 9: "Actus intellectus assentientis veritati divinae ex imperio voluntatis a Deo motae per gratiam." Note that this definition of faith is the one given in the *Catechism of the Catholic Church* (155). The corresponding definition of faith is: "Faith is a habit of mind, by which eternal life begins in us, making the intellect assent to things that are not apparent" (*QDV* 14, 2).

[11] *Credo*, no. 860.

[12] In Cai, *Super Epistolas S. Pauli*, vol. 1, Romans, no. 108.

[13] *Credo*, no. 861.

[14] 1 Cor 13:12.

[15] Heb 11:6.

[16] Cf. *QDV* 14, 2.

[17] *Super Hebr.*, no. 556.

[18] *Credo*, no. 862.

[19] Ibid.

[20] *ST* II–II, 12, 1 ad 2.

[21] Cf. *Compendium of Theology*, trans. Cyril Vollert (St. Louis, Mo.: Herder, 1952), chap. 2.

²² Cf. *ST* II–II, 4, 6.

²³ *In Boe.* 3, 1 ad 4.

²⁴ *ST* II–II, 2, 9 ad 3.

²⁵ Cf. *Super Evangelium S. Ioannis*, ed. Raphaelis Cai, O.P. (Rome: Marietti, 1952), no. 662: "Three things lead us to faith in Christ. First, natural reason. . . . Second, the testimony of the Law and the Prophets. . . . Third, the preaching of the Apostles and of others"; hereafter cited as *Super Ioan.*

²⁶ Cf. *SCG* II, 40.

²⁷ Cf. *In Boe.* 2, 3.

²⁸ This is the normal path of belief. However, "if someone nourished in such a manner [namely, by brute animals] follows the lead of natural reason in desiring good and fleeing evil, it is to be held with the greatest of certainty that God either would reveal to him those things which are necessary for believing through internal inspiration or would direct some preacher to him, as he sent Peter to Cornelius, *Acts*, c. 10" (*QDV* 14, 11 ad 1).

²⁹ Cf. *SCG* III, 154, where Aquinas calls such signs "argumentum fidei".

³⁰ Cf. *SCG* III, 154.

³¹ Cf. *SCG* I, 6.

³² *ST* II–II, 6, 1.

³³ *ST* II–II, 6, 1, is one of many passages where Aquinas cites Ephesians 2:8: "Faith is the gift of God."

³⁴ Cf. *Super Rom.*, no. 842: "[T]he word of one who speaks exteriorly [for example, a preacher's word] is not a sufficient cause of faith, unless the heart of a man be attracted by the virtue of God speaking interiorly." No. 844: "[T]wo things are required for faith: one of which is the inclination of the heart to believing, and this is not from hearing, but from the gift of grace; the other, however, is the determination of the things to be believed, and this is from hearing."

³⁵ *Super Rom.*, nos. 62 and 105.

³⁶ The belief of the devils is not meritorious because they do not believe out of an ordering of the will to the good but because the intellect is convinced by signs (see *ST* II–II, 5, 2).

³⁷ *ST* II–II, 6, 1 ad 3.

³⁸ Cf. *SCG* III, 154: "So, it was necessary for the oral teaching of the preachers to be confirmed by certain signs, whereby it might be plainly shown that this oral teaching came from God; so, the preachers did such things as healing the sick, and the performance of other difficult deeds, which only God could do. Hence, the Lord, sending forth his disciples to preach, said in Matthew (10:8): 'Heal the sick, raise the dead, cleanse the lepers, cast out devils.'" Cf. also *ST* III, 43, 1.

³⁹ *Super Ioan.*, nos. 1569, 1570.

⁴⁰ *Super Ioan.*, no. 319.

⁴¹ *Super Ioan.*, no. 662.

[42] *In Boe.* 3, 1 ad 4. The simple, however, are not to be blamed if they are led astray as to subtle points of faith: "[N]o one should ever be tested about something he is not obliged to believe explicitly. Yet at times even the unlettered are put to the test about minute points of faith. Thus everyone is held to believe everything explicitly. Further, if simple people are not obliged to an explicit faith, it must be that they have an implicit faith in what their teachers believe. This, however, is risky, since the teachers might fall into error. Even ordinary people, then, would seem bound to an explicit faith. Thus all men alike are bound to an explicit faith" (*ST* II–II, 2, 6 ad 2 and ad 3).

[43] Cf. *ST* II–II, 5, 3: "The formal objective of faith is the first truth as this is made known in Scripture and in Church teaching. Anyone, therefore, who does not hold as the infallible and divine rule of faith Church teaching that derives from divine truth as handed down in Scripture, does not have the habit of faith. He accepts things of faith in a way other than by faith." Cf. *QDV* 14, 10 ad 10.

[44] Cf. *ST* II–II, 1, 1 and *QDV* 14, 8 ad 2.

[45] *ST* II–II, 1, 7. Cf. *Super Ioan.*, no. 1004 (Jn 6:70), where Aquinas names the Trinity and the Incarnation as being the principal objects of belief.

[46] III *Scriptum super Sententiis* (Paris: Lethielleux, 1956), p. 769, dist. xxiv, art. 2, sol. 2. Hereafter cited as *Sent.*

[47] *QDV* 14, 10 ad 7. Note that "the size of a dime" is a free translation of "diameter sit asimeter costae", which literally means "its diameter is like in measure to one's rib." Cf. *In Boe.* 3, 1 ad 5: "Taken one way, what is outside of reason can signify defect; . . . taken in another way, it can signify what exceeds, as when man is led by divine grace to that which is above reason—and thus to live outside of reason is not bad for man but is a good above man. And such is the knowledge of things that belong to the faith; although even the faith itself is not outside of reason in every mode. For this natural reason holds: that those things which are said by God ought to be assented to."

[48] Cf. *In Boe.* 2, 3, and II *SCG*, art. 3.

[49] *QDV* 14, 10 ad 8.

[50] *In Boe.* 2, 3. In addition to the preambles to the faith, another thing that may precede faith is the establishment of the authority of the one claiming to announce the true faith. As noted above, natural reason is to be used in regard to this latter as well (cf. *SCG* I, 6: "the faithful do not believe lightly"). Note that while the preambles are demonstrable by natural reason, the arguments adduced to establishing the Church's authority are not: "[A]rguments which compel one toward the faith, such as miracles, do not per se prove the faith but prove the truthfulness of the one announcing the faith. And therefore they do not cause certain knowledge (*scientiam*) of the things which pertain to the faith" (III *Sent.*, dist. xxiv, art. 2, sol. 2 ad 4)

[51] Cf. III *Sent.*, dist. xxv, q. 2, sol. 1 ad 1.

[52] *SCG* I, 4.

[53] Cf. *ST* II–II, 2, 10 ad 2.

[54] *ST* II–II, 2, 10.

[55] Cf. *In Boe.* 2, 3: Secondly, [reason is useful] for making those things which belong to the faith known through certain similitudes, as Augustine uses many similitudes drawn from philosophical teachings for the purpose of manifesting the Trinity in his books on the Trinity.

[56] *Compendium of Theology*, chap. 36.

[57] Aquinas acknowledges that it can be known through natural reason that divine providence governed the world. Still, a person who did know this could believe in the providence of God as revealed by the faith: "For the truth that God is includes everything that we believe to exist eternally in God and that will comprise our beatitude. *Faith in God's providence comprises all those things that God arranges in history for man's salvation and that make up our way towards beatitude.*" (*ST* II–II, 1, 7; emphasis mine). For the reason for many things ordered by God in view of man's salvation cannot be discovered through natural reason (cf. *Super Matt.*, nos. 950, 951).

[58] Cf. *Super Hebr.*, no. 99: "The chief portent is that God became man. Isaiah 8:18: 'I and the boys whom God gave me are portents', namely, that I am man and that the boys believe in me. For it was a wonder that the human heart could believe this."

[59] In Cai, *Super Epistolas S. Pauli*, vol. 1, 1 Corinthians, no. 47.

[60] Cf. III *Sent.*, dist. xxiv, art. 3, qla. 3, sc, p. 773: "Through human reasonings the faith is elucidated. But eternal life is promised to the one elucidating [it], as is manifest from Eccli. 24:31: 'They who elucidate me will have eternal life': which would not be if through such elucidation the merit of faith would be diminished. Furthermore, to the extent that a virtue is nearer to the end, to that extent it is more meritorious. But the end of the faith is the understanding of the truth to which man draws near through human reasonings. Therefore human reason does not diminish the merit of faith but augments it."

[61] *ST* III, 1, 2.

[62] *SCG* I, 9.

[63] Cf. *SCG* I, 8 and 9.

[64] *In Boe.* 2, 3, sc.

[65] Cf. *In Librum Beati Dionysii de Divinis Nominibus Expositio* (Rome: Marietti, 1950), no. 7: "In the doctrine of the faith we are not able to rely upon principles of human wisdom."

[66] *ST* I, 1, 5 ad 2.

[67] *In Boe.* 2, 3. Cf. II *SCG*, art. 3.

[68] See *SCG* II, 3, which shows that knowledge of creatures is of value in destroying errors concerning God. We might note in passing that knowledge of creatures through natural reason is not only helpful to faith but is conducive to love: "First, because meditation on his works enables us in some measure to admire and reflect upon his wisdom. . . . Secondly, this consideration [of God's

works] leads to admiration of God's sublime power, and consequently inspires in men's hearts reverence for God. . . . Thirdly, this consideration incites the souls of men to the love of God's goodness" (*SCG* II, 2).

[69] *In Boe.* 2, 1.

[70] *In Boe.* 2, 3.

[71] Note that in the matters in which there is overlap as to the conclusions drawn by faith and those drawn by natural reason, the argumentation of each proceeds according to different principles.

[72] Aquinas does not use the words "science" and "scientist" in the same way we do nowadays. Nonetheless, it is plain that Aquinas maintains that the sort of questions we call scientific shed relatively little light on matters of the faith.

[73] *SCG* II, art. 4.

[74] *ST* I, 70, 1 ad 3.

[75] *SCG* I, 7.

[76] Cf. Aristotle, *Politics* 1335b20.

[77] *In Boe.* 3, 1 ad 3.

[78] Cf. Mt 19:8.

[79] *ST* I–II, 100, 1.

[80] *QDV* 14, 11 2nd ad 3. Cf. also *ST* I, 79, 12.

[81] Aquinas does not hesitate to call ethics and politics, to which ethics is subordinated, genuine sciences. See *Commentary on the Nicomachaean Ethics*, trans. C. I. Litzinger, O.P., vol. 1 (Chicago: Regnery, 1964). "He says political science is the most important, not simply, but in that division of practical sciences which are concerned with human things, the ultimate end of which political science considers. The ultimate end of the whole universe is considered in theology which is the most important without qualification. He says that it belongs to political science to treat the ultimate end of human life. This however he discusses here since the matter of this book covers the fundamental notions of political science." Further, see no. 113: "In this work the Philosopher speaks of happiness as it is attainable in this life, for happiness in a future life is entirely beyond the investigation of reason."

[82] *QDV* 14, 2.

[83] *In Boe.* 2, 3: "As, however, Sacred Doctrine is founded upon the light of faith, so philosophy is founded upon the natural light of reason. Whence it is impossible that those things which pertain to philosophy be contrary to those things which pertain to the faith, but they fall short of them."

[84] *QDV* 14, 11 ad 2. Cf. also ibid. ad 1 (cited in an earlier note).

[85] *Acts* 10.

[86] Lk 7.

[87] *Super Ioan.* 2, 3.

[88] Those Catholic philosophers who study ethics must take pains to avoid the pitfall of adopting a theological mode when doing so. For example, some

mistakenly begin a discussion of human law from the theological viewpoint of its being a participation of eternal law rather than from everyday experience of living under law. Those who neglect examining moral experience are ineffectual in debates with others who, although mistaken as to their conclusions, do approach morality on the basis of natural reason.

[89] For this reason, strictly speaking, there is no such thing as "Christian philosophy". All philosophy consists of logical arguments ultimately based on first principles naturally known. Thus Saint Thomas never uses the expression "Christian philosophy" (nor incidentally does *Aeterni Patris*). The expression "Christian philosopher", meaning a philosopher who avails himself of the advantage of the extrinsic measure afforded him by the faith, is less misleading.

[90] *Super Ioan.*, nos. 1197–99.

John M. Haas

THE RELATIONSHIP OF
NATURE AND GRACE
IN SAINT THOMAS

The question of the relationship between nature and grace in the thought of Saint Thomas has provided the fuel for countless theological controversies since the thirteenth century. They surfaced in the middle of this century with particular vehemence as a result of the *nouvelle théologie* of Henri de Lubac. I would like to avoid any discussion of those controversies, which would make it virtually impossible to address the topic at hand.

Also, the question of the relation of nature and grace in Saint Thomas enters into every aspect of dogmatic and moral theology, for one is talking of nothing less than the redemption of man. Since I obviously cannot address all the issues associated with the subject in question, I will simply discuss those elements of the topic which I believe are particularly illuminating in understanding the thought of Saint Thomas and also which are of particular importance for living the Christian life today.

Since I am a professor of moral theology, it is not surprising that I have chosen Saint Thomas' teaching on the virtues as the starting point for this discussion. I do so because the teaching of the Angelic Doctor on the virtues reveals his philosophical anthropology, that is, his understanding of the nature of man, the one who needs to be redeemed and, indeed, has been redeemed by Jesus Christ.

I do not want to venture into still another area of great controversy, which has to do with the question of whether there ever was such a thing as *"natura pura"*, or "pure human nature". One has to question whether there ever was such a thing as "pure human nature", since Saint Thomas and the tradition have taught that our first parents were created by God and then endowed with preternatural gifts, such as "integrity", which meant that their lower appetites, such as those ordered toward food and sex, were always perfectly under the direction of their intellect and will. When our first parents sinned, they lost those preternatural gifts and became subject to their "fallen nature". Consequently, there are those theologians who argue that there has never been "pure human nature"; there have only been human nature with the preternatural gifts, fallen human nature, and redeemed human nature.

There is really no need to enter into this controversy to present the thought of Saint Thomas; we merely start with men as we know them in their current historical situation, that is, fallen and subject to sin. But even though they are fallen, they are not totally depraved and incapable of any good deed. Such a concept would have been entirely alien to Saint Thomas. However, we do begin with man deeply wounded even in his highest faculties and powers, the intellect and the will. Rather than the intellect and will directing the lower appetites toward the goods toward which they are naturally ordered, such as food, drink, and sex, they now find themselves terribly buffeted and pulled hither and yon by unruly passions, what has traditionally been termed the disorder of concupiscence.

Saint Thomas takes man as he is, a created nature, and as created, ordered in his very being toward ends given him by his Creator. There have been many who have presented the philosophical anthropology of Saint Thomas in fundamentally, if not purely, Aristotelian terms of faculties and appetites. While Saint Thomas' understanding of the human person is indeed quite similar to that of Aristotle, and quite open to all the insights and advances of modern science about the human animal, there is always a guiding, interpretive Judeo-Christian concept present in Thomas' thought.

Even when the Common Doctor is dealing with man in his pre-baptismal natural life without grace, he does not see man simply as man, but man as "creature". It seems that this understanding of natural man, which is hardly unique to Saint Thomas, is critically important in our own day, which is characterized by atheism, the systematic atheism of socialism and the so-called "practical atheism" of the industrialized and technologically advanced nations. The socialists dismiss any notion of God out of conviction, while the secularists do so usually out of indifference. The socialists attempt to structure a world while fully aware (in their own minds) that there is no God, while the secularists attempt to do so *as if there were no God*. In either case, man suffers.

Man is treated as if he had no intelligible nature reflecting the mind and purposefulness of a Creator. Man, therefore, becomes the "creator" and can fashion himself however he wishes, with no regard for the restraints of a created nature. The political state with such a mind-set does not recognize any objective nature or meaning of individual human beings, who therefore have no rights and come to be used by the state to advance its own interests, often at the expense of individual citizens.

But if man in his natural condition is a creature, he reflects the mind and intentions of the Creator. In fact, there is such a thing as human nature precisely because, and only because, man is created. Saint Thomas says, "to be made and to be created properly belong to whatever has *being*; . . . matter does not exist except by creation; for creation is the production of the whole being."[1]

Man has a human nature precisely because he is created. And he has a nature that is purposeful, which is ordered toward an end, ultimately God himself. As Saint Thomas says, "Every agent acts for an end . . . (and) the divine goodness is the end of all things."[2] Man was created by God and hence bears traces of him. Man was created by God and for him, and consequently all human actions actually seek him. As Thomas expresses it, "All things desire God as their end in desiring any particular good, whether this desire be intellectual or sensible, or natural, that is, without knowledge; for nothing is good and desirable except inasmuch as it participates in the likeness to God."[3]

Man has a nature that is essentially ordered toward ends, the attainment of which are perfective of that nature. Consequently he has rights and obligations. Man is obliged to fulfill his nature and consequently has the right, that is, the moral claim, to those means necessary for the fulfillment of his natural obligations, that is, those means necessary for his self-fulfillment. Man's creatureliness, which is characteristic of him as *natural* man, is the source of his worth and the guarantor of the respect that is due to him from others. And man's creatureliness can be seen and recognized truly only in the concrete, historical human being whom we encounter. As Saint Thomas says in the *Summa Theologiae*: "This very fact that the creature possesses a modified and finite nature makes it clear that it derives from a certain source."[4] That certain source, of course, is God.

However, because man is a creature does not mean that all questions about him must simply be referred back to the Creator. In fact, by virtue of things having been created, they have their own essence, their own nature, which can be studied and known with respect to themselves. We can know things as God has created them, as they are in themselves. As Saint Thomas said in the *Summa Contra Gentiles*, we know things "secundum quod hujusmodi sunt", according to their own mode of being.[5]

This means that there is a certain autonomy (to use a very modern word) with respect to the world in the thought of Saint Thomas. The *saeculum*, or secular order as distinct from the spiritual order, has its own dignity and is not only a worthy sphere for human action but is the one most appropriate for it. The Christian medical researcher can study the reproductive system of the human female with a view toward overcoming various causes of infertility. He need not view it in its intricate complexity as a proof for the existence of God, although it can serve that purpose! He studies it in order to help people in need in the natural order. He studies it in order to advance the purposes of medicine.

The *saeculum*, or the natural order, is distinct from the spiritual order but is not separated from it and is certainly not opposed to it. One of the errors that arose in much Protestant thought, and persists to our own day even in secular culture, is that the natural and supernatural orders are opposed to one another. Because of the doctrine of the total depravity of man, classical Protestantism tends to look at fallen man as radically over against God.[6] In the classical Protestant theory of justification, man is never truly made righteous. God merely regards him as righteous by virtue of the saving actions of Jesus Christ performed on his behalf. Man is treated by God only as though he were righteous, that is, he has righteousness *imputed* to him. Man remains a depraved sinner even as he is justified, which is the Protestant doctrine of *simul justus et peccator*, that is, one is justified, treated as just, even though he remains a sinner.[7]

As a result of this erroneous thinking, there has developed in the general Protestant/secular culture the perception that nature and grace, nature and supernature, the profane and the sacred, the secular and the religious are opposed to one another. While this mistaken thinking has profoundly influenced even some Catholic thinkers, it is a notion that is profoundly un-Catholic. Even though an infinite gap separates the Creator from the creature, as articulated in the thought of Saint Thomas, they are not in opposition to one another.

The *saeculum*, or the natural order, is distinct from the spiritual, but it is not separated from it. In the hierarchy of being, the natural is ordered toward the supernatural so that it never loses any of its own proper, distinct, and unique created essence, derived from the Creator himself.

As Saint Thomas puts it:

[I]n the parts of the universe every creature exists for its own
proper act and perfection, and the less noble for the nobler, as
those creatures that are less noble than man exist for the sake of
man, while each and every creature exists for the perfection of
the entire universe. Furthermore, the entire universe, with all its
parts, is ordained toward God as its end, inasmuch as it imitates,
as it were, and shows forth the divine goodness, to the glory of
God. Reasonable creatures, however, have in some special and
higher manner God as their end, since they can attain to him
by their own operations, by knowing and loving him. Thus it is
plain that the divine goodness is the end of all corporeal things.[8]

It is the divine goodness that orders all things to itself even
as it transcends them. This understanding is the very antithesis
of one based on the notion of opposition. This insight is very
important for a proper understanding of the relation of nature
and grace in Thomas' thought.

Man is ordered toward those ends for which God has created him. Indeed, we can say that the eternal law is the mind
of God ordering all things, including men, toward their created ends. However, in the material, created order, man has a
unique dignity. He can see and understand the ends toward
which he is ordered and can consciously act in accord with
them by choosing actions that are appropriate for the attainment of his created ends.

Lower animals, of course, do not have this capacity. They act
by instinct, without awareness, achieving the ends for which
they were created. The male and female Boxer dogs that we
once had were ordered in their sexual complementarity toward the propagation of the species. When the female came
into heat, the two of them did not reflect on the significance
of this but simply acted instinctively, bringing about a litter
of eight pups. By acting as they did by instinct, our Boxers
conformed themselves to God's eternal law.

Human beings are also subject to the eternal law, but in a
different way. In some ways, they are no more free than the
Boxers. I have just finished a bowl of soup, and my stomach

has begun to digest it without any command from me. However, what constitutes characteristically human behavior is that behavior which I choose. I did not want to eat too much soup, for if I did, I would become sleepy as I digested it, making it more difficult to do my work. So, in spite of the fact that I was still hungry, I ate no more soup so that I could more effectively carry on my distinctively human activity, thinking and choosing and working, for which I ultimately consumed soup in the first place.

A young man on the Jersey shore in the springtime may see a young lady, the very sight of whom will engender cardiovascular and hormonal responses in him similar to those to which our male Boxer was subject. However, the young man will understand the ultimate purposes lying behind those physiological changes taking place in him. He will understand they are fundamentally ordered toward coupling, and coupling is ordered toward procreation and bonding with another human being. And he will understand that the engendering of new life entails a responsibility for the nurture of that life, which requires the institution of the family. And since he is not yet ready to establish a family, he holds in check the physiological changes that have begun to stir within him and does not surrender himself to them. This human awareness of the purposes of God's creative mind and the formulating of principles and commands to direct actions is what the natural moral law is all about. As Saint Thomas says, "The natural law is nothing other than the rational creature's participation in the eternal law."[9]

Saint Thomas saw clearly that human nature has certain inclinations that are ordered toward particular ends. As man perceives the ends toward which these inclinations are ordered, he makes choices that are apt for the attainment of those ends. But these appetites for the good are not always focused and properly oriented in the choices of intermediate goods that themselves ought to be ordered toward the attainment of man's end. It is necessary to shape and orient these appetites so that choices of those goods that are appropriate to the attainment of man's true end come to be made with increasing ease. Once a man has so shaped his appetite through right choices, we say that he has attained a habit that enables him to achieve his end well.

Saint Thomas quotes Aristotle to the effect that "a habit is a disposition whereby one is disposed well or ill."[10] If the set disposition is one that enables us to achieve our ends well, it is called a virtue. If it disposes poorly to the attainment of our ends, we refer to it as a vice. Virtues are simply good habits and vices bad habits that have resulted from repetitious actions and that, once formed, are very difficult to change.

This is all very well known. What might be rather less known, and, indeed, may be a bit surprising, are some of the other things that Saint Thomas also refers to as habits, such as health and beauty.[11] How is health a habit? It certainly is not a set disposition resulting from repetitious acts. This can be seen all the more clearly in beauty. Strain and exercise as I might, I cannot make myself beautiful if I am not. Now health and beauty are indeed qualities that help one attain one's ends more easily, but they seem to be qualities that are more foundational to our existence than the qualities that arise from our actions. They seem to touch, in a sense, our very being out of which our operational virtues arise. Since habit is ordered to action, how can health or beauty be called habits? Saint Thomas tells us, "Health is said to be a habit, or a habitual disposition, in relation to nature. . . . But in so far as nature is the principle of an act, [even health] consequently implies a relation to an act."[12]

In other words, a man acts in accord with his nature. A man acts as a man. If he is healthy, he will be able to perform those actions characteristic of his nature with greater ease. We see here a distinction between what might be called an "entitative habit", or quality touching upon the very being or nature of the agent, and operative habits, which are the perfections of inclinations resulting from the repetition of wholesome actions and which are also known as virtues.

These distinctions are important for our understanding of the relation between nature and grace because they are very helpful in our gaining some understanding of the operation of grace upon us and what effect it has on our natural faculties and appetites or inclinations. One of the most important truths of the Christian life, and one that has always been unambiguously and forcefully taught by the Catholic Church, is the fact that grace does not destroy nature but rather builds upon it, perfects and elevates it. As Saint Thomas says: "The gifts of grace are added to nature in such a way that they do not destroy but rather perfect nature. Thus the light of faith which is infused in us by grace does not destroy the natural light of reason divinely given to us."[13]

Despite his treatment of the life of virtue, which strikes some Protestant Christians as being too optimistic about the capabilities of man, Saint Thomas is keenly aware that man is incapable of living the moral life without the help of divine grace. The only kinds of individuals Saint Thomas knew personally, of course, were fallen men and redeemed men. He obviously never knew the "integral men" who were our first parents in the Garden of Eden, endowed with preternatural gifts. Likewise he never knew a "purely natural" man ordered toward and capable of fulfillment in the natural order with no need for redemption. As far as we know, such a man has never existed. Thomas knew only fallen man and redeemed man. And fallen man could have the image of God in him restored to its pristine beauty only with the help of God.

But in restoring and elevating man, God would not destroy his humanity in the process. God created men to be men. When man is restored, he is elevated in his nature. He does not become something other than man. He does not become an angel, for example. But as man is restored in his humanity, he is at the same time elevated by God beyond anything he could ever have imagined or hoped for. God ennobles man and capacitates him to become a sharer in his own divine nature. Saint Thomas is in awe of this mighty act of God and recognizes that we could never expect it or ever come to know of it were it not for the gift of God in Jesus Christ shown to us in divine revelation. Through grace we are elevated to a life we could never attain through our own natural powers. And once we are elevated to this new life, we will need new capacities, new powers, to attain the new end of the divine life to which we are now ordered.

Actions flow from a nature. We have become new creatures who need new powers. It is sanctifying grace that will effect this change in us. The divine life will touch and transform us in such a way that we will become much more than we could ever become by our own power. We will become children of God. We will become coheirs with Christ of all that the Father has prepared for his only begotten Son. Thomas reminds us, "By grace we are born again sons of God."[14] And this is a true rebirth that touches upon our very nature, upon our very being. Since action follows upon being, something must occur to our very being if we are going to live the new life to which we have been called as adopted children of God.

And something does happen. We are touched and transformed by sanctifying grace. We undergo an ontological transformation. After it has occurred, we are no longer what we simply were previously. As Thomas says, "generation terminates at the essence prior to the power. Therefore grace is in the soul's essence prior to being in the powers." And elsewhere, "[It] remains that grace, being prior to virtue, has therefore a subject prior to the powers of the soul, so that it is in the essence of the soul. . . . [T]hrough the nature of the soul does [man] participate in the divine nature, after the manner of a likeness, through a certain regeneration or re-creation."[15]

Saint Thomas understands the awesomeness of such an act. The rather complacent attitude toward God expressed in such popular expressions of God as "the man upstairs" or "our copilot" border on the blasphemous. The re-creation and rebirth of one sinner is, Saint Thomas reminds us, greater than the creation of the entire cosmos out of nothing, including the creation of those beings who rank in the created order above men, the angels. Thomas approvingly quotes Saint Augustine on this point: "Let him that can, judge whether it is greater to create the angels just than to justify the ungodly. Certainly, if they both betoken equal power, one betokens greater mercy."[16]

Thomas tells us that the justification of the sinner is the greatest of God's works. "A work may be called great in two ways", Thomas tells us. "First, on the part of the mode of action, and thus the work of creation is the greatest work, wherein something is made from nothing; secondly, a work may be called great on account of what is made, and thus the justification of the ungodly, which terminates at the eternal good of a share in the Godhead, is greater than the creation of heaven and earth, which terminates at the good of the mutable nature."[17] Thomas quotes various Scriptures in his works to remind us that we have become "as gods" through the effects of God's grace.[18]

The sanctifying grace that transforms us is also called "habitual grace" by Saint Thomas because it touches our very being in a way that is analogous to the habit of health or beauty. Sanctifying grace disposes or capacitates us to perform actions of which we would otherwise be incapable. There is the tendency for us to understand the concept of habit solely in terms of the means by which we acquire the habit. But a habit is one thing, Thomas makes clear, and the means by which we acquire the habit another.

I have the acquired habit of speaking English, which resulted from years of practice. In other words, I have the set disposition to speak English with facility. That is the habit. The way I acquired the habit can be seen in the way in which my young children acquire their habit of speech. Two- or three-year-old children can drive their parents to distraction with the incessant repetition of new words they hear. But what they are doing is acquiring the habit of speech.

Now even though I have never acquired the facility of speaking Chinese and would have to work very hard at acquiring it,

God *could* grant me the gift of tongues, so that I could immediately begin speaking Chinese. And the set disposition, the
habit, or *habitus*, of speaking Chinese, would be just as surely
mine as if I had had to work for it over many years.

This is analogous to what happens when sanctifying grace
operates upon us and bestows upon us a new supernatural quality. I now have the capacity, the settled disposition, to perform
supernatural acts of which I would otherwise be totally incapable. But that capacity, that *habitus*, was simply bestowed upon
me. I did not gain it through repetitious acts, since no number
of natural actions could possibly enable me to perform actions
that are simply beyond my nature. This *habitus*, this new capacity for living a supernatural life, is an entirely free gift bestowed
upon me by God. But because it is bestowed upon me by God
rather than acquired by me does not make it any less a *habitus*,
that is, a set disposition by which I can act so as to attain my
ends. Now, however, once I have been reborn through God's
grace in the waters of baptism, I am granted new ends, which
are supernatural. My end is now no longer simply the good,
well-ordered, virtuous life in community (which is wondrous
enough), but rather my end is now the divine life of the community of Persons of the Blessed Trinity itself and of all the
friends of God, human and angelic, in heaven.

If I am given this new end for my life, I must also be given
the virtues or operative habits to live such a life. And these
virtues by which we can now perform supernatural acts are
faith, hope, and love. As Saint Thomas tells us: "The theological virtues direct man to supernatural happiness in the same
way as by the natural inclination man is directed to his connat-
ural end."[19] These new powers perfect, not an angelic person,
but a human person. Faith is a perfecting and an elevating of
reason, for example, so that I can now give intellectual assent
to truths of the supernatural order of which any natural human
would simply be incapable.

No mere human being could possibly look at the first-
century Palestinian carpenter and itinerant rabbi known as Jesus

of Nazareth and declare, "You are the Christ, the son of the living God!" No one could look upon this laborer with calloused hands and perspiring forehead, this carpenter with dirty feet covered with wood shavings, this workman whose tunic smelled of fish after helping his friends empty their nets, this laborer slumped against the wall sitting on the bench in the workshop, exhausted after a hard day's work, no one could look upon such a man and declare him to be—God, the Mighty and Immortal One, the second Person of the eternal Trinity through whom and by whom all things came to be. No mere man could make such a claim. Such an affirmation can be made only by one who has been capacitated by God to make supernatural acts.

This is what our Lord meant when he said to Peter after his profession of faith, "Blessed are you, Simon Bar-Jonah! No mere man has revealed this to you, but my Father who is in heaven."[20]

God's gift of faith enables us to make such supernatural acts as acknowledging the divine nature of Christ. Faith, like grace, is a free gift from God, which we cannot acquire and which we certainly do not deserve.

Even though faith, hope, and charity are known as the theological virtues because they enable us to act directly for God (*theos*) as our end, they really have more in common with faculties than they do with operative virtues. A faculty is a human capacity to perform a certain kind of action. An operative virtue, on the other hand, is a good habit that has been developed in us by repeated actions. For instance, in the natural order, the ability or capacity to speak is a faculty given to me by God. I am born with it. My ability to speak English, on the other hand, is comparable to an operative virtue. The faculty of speech had to be perfected and "set" through my repeated efforts, so that I now speak English effortlessly.

The theological virtues are called "virtues" because they have to do with human actions, for example, making an act of faith or belief in God, making an act of hope, and so forth.

However, they are more like faculties in that they are a gift from God that alone gives us the capacity to make acts of faith, hope, or love. Without them, we could not make these acts. That is why we say the theological *virtues* are also similar to *faculties*.

It ought not to be surprising that there is not an exact correspondence on the supernatural level with the human powers and faculties on the natural. As the Council of Orange declared, "The supernatural is so far beyond the natural that the dissimilarities between the two are greater than the similarities when we speak by analogy." This is so because there is an unbridgeable gap between the Creator and the creature, so that we can only speak of the Creator by observing the effects of his actions and by making use of the language of analogy. This is true even when it comes to the divine life we come to share with him in Christ. Faith, hope, and charity enable us to perform supernatural acts and so, as said above, appear to have more the character of faculties, even as they are called virtues because they pertain to human action.

This understanding of the relation of nature and grace leads to certain conclusions. When we do not have sanctifying grace within us, we are simply incapable of leading a supernatural existence. This is why Saint Thomas refers to sanctifying grace as habitual grace. We are either with a habit or without a habit. If we are without the habit, we cannot perform the actions that properly flow from that habit, or established disposition. Consequently, any grievous action against our friendship with God, any repudiation of that relationship, will lead to the loss of the life of God within us, will lead, in other words, to the loss of sanctifying grace. Because we cannot acquire the established disposition of sanctifying grace in the first place, even so we cannot restore it ourselves. Sanctifying grace can only be restored through the means that God himself has established, namely, the sacrament of penance and reconciliation or a perfect act of contrition ordered toward that sacramental channel of grace.

THE RELATIONSHIP OF NATURE AND GRACE

When the habit of sanctifying grace, the principle of the divine life within us, is absent, there is merely the state or condition of supernatural death. In other words, we are no longer disposed toward the performance of supernatural acts. Indeed, we cannot perform them at all. We can perform actions that can be judged on the natural order to be good and virtuous, perhaps, but they no longer have a meritorious effect on the supernatural level.

Because habitual grace is lost through mortal sin, there is in its place habitual sin. One has gone from a state of being divinized, from being as God, to a state of being fallen again. The habit or capacity for performing supernatural acts has been replaced with the habit of being incapable of performing supernatural acts. When today one reads a moral theology manual from a couple of generations ago that speaks of a sinner being in a state of habitual sin, one thinks that the sinner is habituated to a certain kind of behavior as a result of repetitious acts. However, this is not at all what the texts meant. One in habitual sin is one who is in a state of unrepented sin. Without repentance and the sacrament of reconciliation, the sinner is incapable of regaining habitual grace, which would enable him once again to perform supernatural acts. In our day, we think of the human condition solely in psychological terms, without making the ontological distinctions seen in Thomas' discussion of habit and habitual grace, and consequently no longer have as sound an understanding of the relation between nature and grace, between the moral life and the sacramental life.

When we commit a mortal sin against friendship with God, we are reduced to the state of being without the grace that capacitates the new life; we are without habitual grace and are in a state of habitual sin, even if, as stated, the sin was committed only once. Only God can restore us to the supernatural life, which he has determined to do through the sacrament of reconciliation.

The fact that habitual grace refers to a capacity given by God rather than a perfected ability resulting from repetitious acts can be seen in the fact that the infant receives habitual, justifying grace in baptism. The infant is incapable of performing any actions that would lead to the acquisition of a habit, yet he is granted the habit of sanctifying grace and the virtues of faith, hope, and love, as the faculties that will enable him to live the Christian life, by the power of the sacrament that works upon him.

As Saint Thomas says in his *Commentary on the First Letter of Paul to the Corinthians*: "God is said to dwell spiritually as in his intimate habitation in the saints whose souls are capable of possessing him by knowledge and of delighting in him through love, even when they are not actively knowing and loving, providing that they have the *habitus* of faith and charity, as is evidently the case in infants that have been baptized."

Without the sanctifying grace received in baptism, we would be able to do nothing on the supernatural order. As Thomas points out: "Man by his natural endowments could will and do the good proportioned to his nature, which is the good of acquired virtue; but he could not do the good that exceeded his nature, which is the good of infused virtue."[21] This infused virtue is received only with sanctifying grace, the principle of a new life in Christ.

Still more conclusions must be drawn from the understanding of the relationship of grace to nature that has been delineated here. Of fundamental importance is the fact that we cannot save ourselves. Grace and faith and the other supernatural powers that we receive are gifts from God to enable us to live the life to which we have been called through baptism. We are no more able to bring about this second birth than we were able to bring about the first birth from our mother's womb.

Thomas also quotes Saint Augustine to the effect that the supernatural virtues are *in nobis, sine nobis*. They are "in us, but without us". Grace and the virtues are truly within us, transforming us into supernaturalized creatures. Grace and righteousness are not merely imputed to us, as the classical Protes-

THE RELATIONSHIP OF NATURE AND GRACE   75

tants would claim. We are not simply treated by God as though
we were righteous; we are made righteous. We are transformed
by grace into truly new creatures. However, the supernatural
virtues are ours, but *sine nobis*, without us. Since we did not
bring the supernatural life about within us, we cannot increase
it within ourselves by ourselves. And we cannot restore it to
ourselves by ourselves.

Through this teaching we see the necessity of the sacraments
of baptism and reconciliation for the life of grace. To deny this
is to suggest that we do not need God, that we can save ourselves, a notion that is repugnant to any follower of Christ.

However, Saint Thomas' understanding of the life of grace,
while it here may appear virtually Protestant with its insistence
on *sola gratia* and *sola fides*, "grace alone" and "faith alone",
is profoundly scriptural and hence significantly different from
the Protestant approach. Saint Thomas truly believes the many
passages in Scripture that tell us to run the race so as to win
the prize,[22] which tell us to pummel and discipline our bodies
so that we might win the victor's wreath,[23] to use our talents
in such a way that they increase and can be returned a hun-
dredfold to the Master when he returns.[24]

And the consequence of this fidelity to scriptural testimony
is the doctrine of "merit", which is found in the Catholic tradition and explained by Saint Thomas. The Christian is able to
perform meritorious acts that permit him to lay claim to the
rewards that have been promised him. The classical Protestant
recoils from the teaching on merit because it appears to un-
dermine the truth of the gratuity of grace. But Saint Thomas
anticipated this antipathy and, indeed, could understand the
truth of it. He writes: "The gift of grace can be considered
. . . in the nature of a gratuitous gift, and thus it is manifest
that all merit is repugnant to grace, since, as the Apostle says
(Rom 11:6), *if by grace, it is not now by works.*" However, this
is a consideration merely of first grace, justifying grace. Since
such grace exceeds the proportion of human nature, it cannot
be merited by actions proportioned by human nature. But the

man transformed by justifying grace is now granted new power and enabled to perform supernatural actions that are actions of God himself, who now dwells in him. As Saint Paul says, "It is no longer I who live, but Christ who lives in me."[25] The truth is that the Thomistic, Catholic teaching of merit is an aspect of the teaching on the gratuity of grace. And there is no thorough understanding of the Catholic life without an understanding of and appreciation for the doctrine of merit.

Saint Thomas explains, "In the state of corrupted nature man needs [a gratuitous strength superadded to natural strength] for two reasons, in order to be healed and, furthermore, in order to carry out works of supernatural virtue, which are meritorious."[26] Every good and noble act we perform out of love of God, explicitly or implicitly, while we are in a state of grace merits a reward from God.

Once we have become children of God we must live as children of God. *Agere sequitur esse*; action follows on being. We act now in accord with our new nature. This is the significance of Christ's teaching on his being the vine and his followers the branches, drawing their life and their fruitfulness from him.[27]

Protestants fear the Catholic teaching on merit is one of sinful presumption. To them we Catholics appear to presume to place God in our debt by performing good works and then laying claim to a reward. But there is no notion of supernatural reward for the man who has not been elevated by divine grace to life in Christ. And it is God himself who establishes the conditions of the relationship. God, the faithful and just One, has promised a reward to those who persevere. Thomas tells us, "Eternal life is granted by God in accordance with the judgment of justice, according to 2 Timothy 4:8: 'As to the rest, there is laid up for me a crown of justice, which the Lord, the just judge, will render to me in that day.' Therefore man merits eternal life."[28]

It is God who binds himself through his own promises. We do not bind him. But once God has promised, he is faithful to his word. If I perform good deeds in Christ, which are therefore proportioned to a supernatural reward, that is, if I am in a state of grace that makes me capable of such deeds, I may then lay claim to the rewards God himself has promised.

Without Christ, we can do nothing; with Christ, we can perform actions that infinitely surpass even moving mountains. As Thomas says:

> If we speak of a meritorious work inasmuch as it proceeds from the grace of the Holy Spirit moving us to eternal life, it is meritorious of eternal life. . . . For thus the value of its merit depends upon the power of the Holy Spirit moving us to eternal life, according to John 4:14: "Shall become in him a fount of water springing up into life everlasting." Furthermore, the worth of the work depends on the dignity of grace, whereby man, being made a partaker of the divine nature, is adopted as a son of God, to whom the inheritance is due by right of adoption, according to Romans 8:17: "If sons, heirs also".[29]

The problem with much Protestantism is not its appeal to Scripture but its selective appeal to Scripture. No Martin Luther or John Calvin can best Thomas Aquinas in his use of and fidelity to Scripture.

When we do not live as the children of God, to which status we have been elevated through a second birth, we then violate our supernaturalized nature. As Saint Thomas says: "To sin is nothing else than to fail in the good that belongs to any being according to its nature."[30] Not to act in accord with our *new* nature as sons and daughters of God is to act beneath the dignity to which we have been raised. We rather colorless human beings surpass in dignity the entire created order that God brought into being out of nothing! Thomas approvingly quotes Saint Augustine "For a just man to be made from a sinner is greater than to create heaven and earth, for heaven and earth shall pass away, but the salvation and the justification of the predestined shall endure."[31]

If we truly considered the dignity to which we have been raised, how much more difficult would sin become. If we truly considered the dignity to which we have been raised, how much more would we be motivated to perform good deeds. We would see them as accomplishing far more than those around us who are not Christians could ever imagine. As Thomas says, "By every meritorious act a man merits the increase of grace, even as he merits the consummation of grace, which is eternal life."[32]

Few things could be more helpful to storing up our treasure in heaven through our actions here on earth, a treasure to which we may one day happily lay claim, than daily to meditate upon our divine filiation. If we truly reflected on who we were, we would have an unsurpassed motive for the moral life. "But eternal life is a good exceeding the proportion of created nature," Saint Thomas tells us, "since it exceeds its knowledge and desire, according to 1 Corinthians 2:9: 'Eye hath not seen, nor ear heard, neither hath it entered into the heart of man.' "[33]

Perhaps this relation of nature and grace in the thought of Saint Thomas could be illustrated with the sacrament of marriage. First of all, marriage is a natural institution. It is common to all peoples and has been present throughout human history. We believe it to have been instituted with the very creation of man and woman in the garden. It involves the totality of the human person as a rational animal, as a rational body. It involves actions that we share with the beasts themselves, actions necessary for the propagation of the species. It involves passions and sexual arousal and intercourse and conception and gestation and bearing of offspring. On the natural level it also involves affection and friendship and toil and frugality and storing up for the future and sacrifice and state agencies and licenses and laws and regulations, since it is natural to human beings to order their lives according to reason. This is a very human activity. Marriage is human nature at its natural best and worst; it is the realm of heroic virtues and base vices. But beyond the natural, marriage can also be the occasion for the supernatural life and for the gaining of merit.

When those who are baptized in Christ, when two children

of God, marry, the institution itself becomes supernaturalized. The gulf between the natural and supernatural is so great that we truly have difficulty even beginning to be able to grasp the significance of God's action through and in us by virtue of our having been graced. But unspeakably wondrous things inevitably occur when the conditions of the supernatural life are in place.

I knew a young woman who was to be married in June to a young man in whose conversion she had been instrumental. She had been his sponsor at his baptism, and her joy that their friendship had borne such spiritual fruit, now culminating in marriage, was boundless. But shortly before the wedding the parish priest was horrified to find out what was causing her such joy; she was about to marry her godson. Regrettably, this is forbidden under Church law. However, it is a prohibition that can be waived by competent ecclesiastical authority. The priest explained that a dispensation would have to be obtained before the wedding could take place. Days of anxious waiting and consternation followed, as they tried desperately to hasten the bureaucratic process. The dispensation was granted in the nick of time.

The young woman was also overjoyed that her sister was going to be able to share in the wedding in a special way by letting her wear the gown in which the sister had been married. But three days before the wedding, the dry cleaners called with the dreadful news that their equipment had malfunctioned and the dress had been destroyed. There was a frantic search for a new gown, and a generous tip had to be offered to have it altered on time.

Were all this not bad enough, the young woman came down with the flu the morning of the wedding and had to recite her vows while her head swam and a cold sweat broke out on her forehead. But even with all these painfully human setbacks, what she and her husband did before the altar was to perform a supernatural act and to bring into being a supernatural reality, the sacrament of matrimony. Through their exchange of vows as baptized sons and daughters of God, they brought into being a bond between the two of them, which for the rest of their lives would allow them to lay claim to, and to receive from, God whatever supernatural help, whatever graces they would need to carry out the arduous and joyous obligations they had just taken upon themselves. And once they had expressed and consummated their vows through a very carnal but for all that supernatural act, intercourse, no power on earth, not that of prince, emperor, or pope—or even of a New York divorce court—could ever destroy that indissoluble bond which God and they had brought about. And the only ones who could ever deny them the blessings and privileges and graces to which that bond entitled them would be themselves, by committing mortal sin, thereby losing the habitual grace that would allow them to receive those gifts.

Here we see no opposition between nature and grace, between the sacred and the profane. Indeed, the sacred comes to permeate the profane even while not destroying it, while still respecting its intrinsic properties. It was always Christian *heretics*, like the Gnostics or Bogomils or Cathars, who thought their being Christian required them to deny the properties of the natural institution of marriage, such as intercourse and its fruit, children. The sacrament of matrimony is the supernaturalizing of a natural institution without destroying the natural, civil institution. After man and woman have become one flesh in Christ so as to share in and reflect to the world his nuptials with his Church, they are empowered to perform actions that far surpass their natural abilities.

Thereafter, the most common of activities become occasions for the growth of grace within the spouses. Doing the dishes or taking out the garbage can become meritorious acts by which they can lay claim to an eternal reward. The enjoyment of the bodily delights of the marriage bed, as they are open to all the goods God intends for them, is an occasion of grace. Helping a daughter with a science project, teaching a son how to keep his eye on the baseball when he swings the bat, are actions of potentially eternal significance. If they are performed by spouses and parents in a state of grace, they have a power and a significance far exceeding the most noble or impressive of human acts without grace.

However, even as these actions have a supernatural significance, there is always a correspondence between the natural and the supernatural. Grace does not destroy nature but perfects and elevates it. The presence of grace in no way eliminates the need for human beings to work and struggle for the attainment of the acquired moral virtues. The husband, for example, may have to refrain from the urge to put two hundred dollars on the football game that night even though he is positive his team is going to win. He can take no chance whatsoever, not even the smallest, that he might lose that money. The family simply needs it too much right now.

The wife must bite her tongue and not badger her husband as he settles into his easy chair for the Monday night football game. He needs time for his own recreation. These are the practice of the simple, moral virtues, and these kinds of naturally virtuous acts must be done if one wants to avoid allowing the natural virtues to weaken, thereby exposing oneself to the risk of being unable to resist later the temptation that might actually lead to the commission of a mortal sin.

Although the supernatural virtues are not increased in us through repetitious acts, the natural, acquired moral virtues are, and the weakening or loss of those virtues can place the entire supernatural life at risk, as they set us up for the fall. We must continue to struggle and to work to develop the natural moral virtues within us. And in so doing we dispose ourselves to an increase in the supernatural virtues necessary for the attainment of our supernatural end. The gratuitousness of grace never means that the struggle for sanctification ends or is not necessary. We cooperate with God's grace, not so we ourselves can bring about an increase of grace within us. We cannot. We do not have that power. We cooperate with God's grace so that we might dispose ourselves toward an increase of grace, which is then granted by God. We do good deeds in and through Christ and gain merit, acquiring a claim to an increase in God's grace. And because he is faithful and just and wants to share his life with us, he grants it.

Saint Thomas draws upon all the rich resources of his received tradition—Hebrew, Greek, Roman, Aristotelian, Neo-platonic, Augustinian, scriptural, and philosophical—to present a clear, systematic, and brightly woven exposition of the relation of nature and grace, overcoming any sense of opposition by seeing all things providentially ordered, on the natural and the supernatural levels, to the divine goodness itself.

NOTES

1 *ST* I, 45, 4.

2 *ST* I, 44, 4.

3 *ST* I, 44, 4 ad 3.

4 *ST* I, 93, 6: "*Hoc ipsum quod creatura habet substantiam modificatam et finita, demonstrat quod sit a quodam principio.*"

5 *SCG* 2, 4 (1).

6 "These two things should be . . . distinctly observed: first, that our nature being so totally vitiated and depraved, we are, on account of this very corruption, considered as convicted and justly condemned in the sight of God, to whom nothing is acceptable but righteousness, innocence, and purity. . . . The other thing to be remarked is that this depravity never ceases in us but is perpetually producing new fruits. . . . For our nature is not only destitute of all good, but is so fertile in all evils that it cannot remain inactive" (John Calvin, *On the Christian Faith*, trans. by John T. McNeill, Library of Liberal Arts [New York: Bobbs-Merrill Company, 1957], pp. 42–43).

7 Cf. Heinrich Schmid, *The Doctrinal Theology of the Evangelical Lutheran Church*, trans. from German and Latin by Charles A. Hay and Henry E. Jacobs, 3d rev. ed. (1875, 1889; reprint, Minneapolis: Augsburg Publishing House, 1961).

8 *ST* I, 65, 2.

9 *ST* I-II, 91, 2.

10 *ST* I-II, 49, 1.

11 Cf. *ST* I-II, 49, 1, and 50, 1.

12 *ST* I-II, 49, 3 ad 3.

13 *Exposition of Boethius' On the Trinity* 2, 3.

14 *ST* I-II, 110, 4.

15 *ST* I-II, 110, 4.

16 *ST* I-II, 113, 9.

17 Ibid.

18 Cf. Ps 84; Ps 145:9; Jn 10:34; Jn 14:12, 2 Pet 1:4.

19 *ST* I-II, 62, 3.

20 Mt 16:17.

21 *ST* I-II, 109, 2.

22 1 Cor 8:24.

23 1 Cor 8:26–27.

24 Mt 25:15ff.

25 Gal 2:20.

26 *ST* I-II, 109, 2.

[27] Jn 15:1ff.
[28] *ST* I–II, 114, 3.
[29] *ST* I–II, 114, 3.
[30] Ibid.
[31] *ST* I–II, 113, 9.
[32] *ST* I–II, 114, 8.
[33] *ST* I–II, 114, 2.

RALPH MCINERNY

THOMAS AQUINAS AND
MORAL RELATIVISM

My subject is Thomas Aquinas and moral relativism. Once when I was asked to address a similar subject, I hit upon the title, "Absolutes, Relatives, and In-laws". It had a serious point. It was meant to distinguish between moral precepts that admit of no exceptions and those that do and to contrast both with legal obligations.

In what follows I will do several things: *first*, recall the bare bones of Thomas' teaching on moral action; second, discuss the most general principles of action, distinguishing between affirmative and negative precepts. I will then suggest that what we call exceptionless principles are likely to be expressed in the negative and that this tells us what the basis for their being exceptionless is. Finally, I will relate this to the Holy Father's magnificent recent encyclical *Veritatis Splendor*.

1. Agents and Moral Action

The mark of the human agent is answerability for what he does. He or others may relevantly ask, "Why are you doing that?" The assumption is that answerability, or responsibility, is of the essence of human action. This in turn presupposes that we might not have done what we did and thus were free to do it. Which is why we are praised or blamed for what we do.

The answer to the question "Why?" is what we had in mind when we acted, the possible act we thought we were executing. It is the mark of the human agent that he knowingly and willingly does what he does. That is why we do not number activities and operations that go on in us involuntarily—digesting, hearing, growing old—among human acts, among responsible acts. We do not ask someone why he is growing bald in the same way that we ask him why he is getting a haircut. The etiology of baldness is known; it has a cause even if I do not cause it. It is not a process initiated—or arrested—by taking thought, something we have on the highest authority.

The question "Why?", addressed to what I am doing, may seem to be less about what I am doing than about some future objective I am thought to have in mind. Thus, when asked what she is doing, Little Iodine can reply that she is clipping off her little brother Orville's ears. This is to explain what she is doing, the deed she is performing. She may again be asked why she is doing that, and she replies that they are playing bullfighter and she is the matador and Orville the bull. And why are they doing that? Because she has been asked to keep Orville out from under the feet of the grown-ups. That is, "Why" can bear either on the object of the act, that which is done, or the end of the act, that for the sake of which it is done. Saint Thomas sometimes calls these the proximate and remote ends of the act.

In recent years, something called action theory has developed, and the question about how to describe an action has been much discussed. Sometimes "the lifting of my hand" is described as a basic act that may support a more or less rich superstructure. Or "the flexing of my finger" is taken as basic, with pulling the trigger, firing the gun, shooting the burglar understood as addenda to the basic act. But "the lifting of my arm" is not a basic *human* act—somebody else may be lifting it; I may have fallen out of a window with the result that my arm goes up as I go down; somebody may just have touched a match to my elbow; and so on. Human acts are those we knowingly and willingly bring about.

What of flexing my finger? I may bring that about, but the

description is not sufficient to appraise it morally. I may be summoning the waiter, testing the wind, or asleep. We would not say that I flex my finger in order to pull the trigger, as if one act led to the other. Pulling the trigger is a fuller description of an action. So, too, is firing the gun: to pull the trigger is to fire the gun—if it is loaded. Shooting the burglar is something we can get our teeth into. My point is a simple one: such progressively more informative descriptions of an action are descriptions of the object of the act, of the proximate end. The various descriptions do not relate to one another as object to remote end but as more or less adequate descriptions of the proximate end or object.

A description of a human act tells us of some deed someone knowingly and willingly does. The description has to be rich enough to permit moral appraisal. "Taking the life of another" is insufficient. We have to know who is doing the taking and whose life is being taken before approving or disapproving. Either way, someone is dead, of course, and that is bad for the one killed, but bad in the way death by an accident is also bad. "Taking the life of an innocent person", on the other hand, describes an action sufficiently for moral disapproval.

"A man and woman mating" insufficiently describes an action so far as moral appraisal goes. "A man mating with a woman not his wife" is sufficient for moral disapproval.

All this may seem to give credence to the notion that philosophical analysis is a species of neurosis. But these are important distinctions, as we shall see, and important for understanding *Veritatis Splendor*'s impatience with the dismissal by some of exceptionless moral norms. Dissenting theologians are usually muddled on the object of the human act.

Object and end are two of the three things Thomas says we must take into account in the moral appraisal of an action —the third is the circumstances. The deed done, the act performed, must be good, and that for the sake of which we do it must also be good. If I take the elbow of a little old lady and guide her across the street, you may want to give me the

Scout's handshake. What I have done is a good thing to do. But if you find that I am delivering her into the hands of greedy heirs who intend to dump her into the East River, you would hastily withdraw your hand.

"What do you have against helping little old ladies?"

An act may have a good object and a bad end or a bad object and a good end, but in either case it will be a bad act. Only when its object, end, and circumstances are good is the act morally good.

2. First Practical Principles

One of Thomas' assumptions about human beings is that they are in agreement on fundamental things both theoretical and practical. This may seem wildly optimistic when you remember your last argument with—well, you fill in the blank. Given the variety and rivalry of views on everything under the sun, it is tempting to see the differences as radical. "We don't have a thing in common." Such sentences are meaningful and true but hyperbolic. Let us imagine that you say tomato and she says tomahto. Imagine a universe in which that is all either of you say. You say tomato, and she says tomahto. But you would agree that in this you differ. In short, there could not be a universe that would consist of only one assertion and its denial: we would also have to add knowledge that the assertion and the denial are not simultaneously true. The disputants have to agree on that in order to disagree: disagreement presupposes agreement. A small point, but it prevents us from thinking that disagreement can be radical or total.

Something similar happens in the practical order, where initially it seems most unlikely. Different judgments about the way things *are* do not have the bite of differences about what we ought or ought not to *do*. Passions are involved, character traits, habits. Our subjective condition seems to play so great a role in practical judgments that it does not seem hyperbolic to say that certain persons are incapable of seeing the truth of a given moral precept. The conditions in which we are brought up, the history of our actions, seem decisive for what we think we should do; and people are brought up in wildly different ways and act accordingly. Communication seems impossible. Nor will we be consoled by the assurance that here, too, both parties will agree that no one could simultaneously hold what divides them. Is there anything practical on which they agree?

Of course there is. Each would allow that whatever he does is done because doing it is better than not doing it. One acts under the assumption that what one is doing is good to do. What does that mean? Good for me to do, good for me, fulfilling of me. As a result of acting thus, I will be better off than I was beforehand—or I would have been worse off if I failed to act. These platitudes about action are taken very seriously by Thomas. Exiguous as the remark is, it is nonetheless true to say that every human agent aims at the good in doing whatever he does.

The difference lies, of course, in what is identified as good. Chesterton said that the young man knocking on the brothel door is looking for God. He has the wrong door, but it is a good and Thomistic point. However mistaken we may be, we are never mistaken about wanting the good. This means that we choose to do what we do because we consider it to be good.

Since everyone can be presumed to want the good, the first task of moral philosophy is to clarify what the true good of human agents is. This is done by noting the pre-moral goods that are already attracting us: self-preservation, food, drink, girls (or boys, if you are a girl), fellowship, society, knowledge. The idea is that these are not things we choose or decide to want —wanting them is built into what we are. That is why I call them pre-moral goods. We are not responsible for being drawn to them.

The objects of such natural inclinations enter into a moral account insofar as I deliberately and voluntarily pursue them

in the light of my integral good. Drink slakes my thirst, and
eating removes the pain of hunger, but when I eat and drink I
am bringing these under the general umbrella of *good-for-me*, a
generality that implies as well that so to pursue them is good
for the kind of agent I am. If for me to eat consists in lunching
on your arm, an invocation of the Golden Rule will make clear
that such an act cannot pass the test. That is why our mothers
always asked us: How would you like it if someone did that to
you? Mothers are the moral teachers of mankind. If we should
formulate a principle to the effect that one ought to eat in a
way that is beneficial to, good for, one, it is difficult to imagine
any gainsayers. The principle is broad enough to encompass
a breach of a diet—something that could be shown, however,
not really to exemplify the principle. A more traditional way
of formulating a basic principle here is, "Be temperate." This
suggests that we ought to pursue pleasurable activities in a way
that does not threaten our overall, general, integral good. If the
things that we want, whether we will to or not, enter into the
account of the integral human good, that integral human good
provides a measure of pursuing the individual goods in an ap-
propriately human way.

Be temperate, be brave, be just, act wisely—the objects of
such precepts are the cardinal virtues. It is universally incum-
bent on everyone to be temperate. This is not to say that I must
always and constantly be performing temperate acts. It applies
semper sed non ubique (always but not everywhere). Negative
precepts—do not commit adultery—are said to apply *semper
et ubique* (always and everywhere). There are times when one
need not perform a temperate act, but there is never a time
when it is okay to commit an injustice.

Exceptionless norms are expressed negatively: they enjoin
us never to perform an act of a certain kind.

Far from having gone out of style, moral absolutes are heard
everywhere. It is not so much a question of whether someone
holds moral absolutes as which ones he holds. Feminists, ecol-
ogists, healthnuts, your mother-in-law, vie with one another in

asserting that there are things that can never be done—smoke, use "man" to mean everyman, kill snaildarters, speak to me in that tone of voice.

The thing to do with moral absolutes, then, is first to ask what the criterion for a precept's being absolute or exceptionless is and then to ask if the various candidates for moral absolutes make the grade.

I propose this criterion. Any deed that is destructive of the integral human good is always and everywhere to be avoided: for example, lying, taking innocent life, adultery, theft. To lie, steal, murder, and commit adultery have long been recognized to be deeds of this kind. Most of the current moral absolutes I referred to earlier manifestly fail this test and thus fail to qualify as true moral absolutes. They are rather the ideological or intimidating attempt to elevate to exceptionless status a kind of conduct that simply cannot bear the weight thereby put upon it.

3. Veritatis Splendor

In his encyclical on Christian morality, the Holy Father makes use of the kind of analysis we have just sketched, one derived from the writings of Saint Thomas Aquinas. Of course, the encyclical does not confine itself to philosophical analysis. Indeed, it is a prolonged meditation on the Gospel story in which the rich young man asks Jesus what he must do in order to be saved (Mt 19:16). The answer is, Keep the commandments, and Jesus goes on to enumerate some of them. When the young man says that he already observes the commandments, Jesus goes on. If you would be perfect, sell all you have, give the proceeds to the poor, and come follow me. The Holy Father sets forth the great moral ideal of the Christian life, which subsumes the commandments taken as natural morality. In recent years, various magisterial documents addressed specific moral problems—contraception, abortion, homosexuality, surrogate parenthood, and so on. Such documents could do little more than indicate the broader moral ideal within which they fit. *Veritatis Splendor* is devoted to recalling that big picture, the Christian answer to the question of the meaning of life. But this big picture enables the Pope to take on the methodologies that underlie the particular errors addressed by earlier documents.

Having recalled the great lines of traditional Catholic moral theory, and the criteria for appraising human acts, the Holy Father takes to task theologians who have called into question exceptionless moral norms. Two bases for rejecting exceptionless norms are given: first, that the object of an act can never be described as something no one may ever do, and, second, that the end or motive of an act is what decides the morality of an act and a good end can trump a bad object. In the fourth part of chapter two of the encyclical, these deviant positions are analyzed and rejected. To reject them is to reject moral relativism.

The response to the encyclical on the part of those who consider themselves the ostensible objects of this criticism has been curious. The Pope, we are told, does not really understand the positions he has criticized. We are told that no moral theologian rejects the notion of exceptionless norms; we are also told that no moral theologian would say that it is sometimes permissible to do something that is morally wrong. Father Richard McCormick has provided us with a survey of many responses to the encyclical.[1] He considers himself to be a target of the encyclical's criticisms and cites many other writers who, like himself, feel that the Pope is simply misinformed on what revisionist moral theologians have been saying.

There is some plausibility in Father McCormick's complaint, but on the whole I think it is disingenuous. The charge is that revisionist theologians have taught that an act that is evil because of its object may nonetheless be permissibly done because of other considerations. The charge is made in terms of the notion of the object of the act that is employed in the encyclical, the notion we have recalled above. The only way in which Father McCormick, on behalf of himself and others, can escape this criticism is by altering and expanding the notion of object. And this is what they have done. Thus they can say that, taking object in their expanded, revisionist sense, they do not teach that when the object is immoral the act can be done for other reasons. The question is not whether the accusation is fair but whether there is any good reason to accept the revised notion of object.

Unfortunately, it is not always clear what this expanded notion is. Revisionists have often misunderstood the traditional notion of object and, indeed, have suggested that the Magisterium employs one sense of object when dealing with questions of sexual morality and quite another in less charged areas. Their claim is that the physical act, the natural occurrence, is taken to be just as such the object of the act. Presumably, this would mean, for example, an act of sexual intercourse considered in a purely biological way. It would be successful or good insofar as it achieved its end, which would be procreation; it would be unsuccessful, a bad instance of the kind, if it failed to do this. To suggest that the Church has been equating good and bad in these senses with morally good or bad is nonsense.

But let Father McCormick provide the setting for the discussion:

> Take an example sometimes cited by opponents of proportionalism: the solitary sex act. This, it is urged, is intrinsically evil from its object. This is the view of the Pope. Proportionalists would argue that this ("solitary sex act") is an inadequate description of the action. For self-stimulation for sperm testing is a different human act from self-pleasuring, much as self-defense is different from homicide during a robbery. They are different because of different reasons for the act, i.e., different goods sought and aimed at different intentions. Intentions tells us what is going on.[2]

The analogy suggested is between (1) "A killing B" and (2) "solitary sex act". Either of these could be described in clinically neutral ways with no mention in the case of (1) of

who A is, why he is doing what he is doing, who B is, and so
forth. (1) could be exemplified by an accident, an execution,
self-defense, a deed done in battle. (1) does not describe a human act, because it does not tell us enough to know who is
accountable for what. As was made clear above, this is commonplace in Thomas and assumed by *Veritatis Splendor.* "A and
B having sexual intercourse" would be similarly shy of having
moral valence. The "solitary sex act" is to be considered in
much the same way. How would it be clinically described?
The stimulation of the genitalia to the point of emission. That
same account would be assumed in speaking of nocturnal emis-
sions, involuntary stimulation while horseback riding, and the
sort of furtive activity some surgeon generals think should be
taught in the schools.

What must be added to (1) and (2) to make them human,
moral acts? They must be deliberately undertaken. They must
be what I propose to do, what I intentionally do. The *successful*
killing of another, the *accomplishment* of an act of intercourse,
does not suffice to make the deliberate doing of them morally
good. (2), when deliberately engaged in, becomes a moral act.
Father McCormick suggests "self-pleasuring" as the analogue
to "homicide" with respect to (1), and "self-stimulation for
sperm testing" as the analogy of "self-defense" with respect
to (1). Like "self-defense" and "homicide," there are different
reasons for acting, that is, different goods sought and different
intentions aimed at. How are these different reasons, goods,
or intentions to be characterized?

One way would be to take them to be some ulterior objective of the act performed, for example, almsgiving done out of
vainglory. Almsgiving might be done out of charity. In either
case, the same moral act, almsgiving, has a proximate end in
view, the object of the act or the proximate end, as Thomas
sometimes calls it. The dispute between revisionists and the
Pope comes down to this: Does the revisionist seek to make
part of the object of the act the ulterior or remote end for
which it may be undertaken, or is he simply making the point

that intention, aim, and so on, may bear on the proximate end as well? If he were doing the latter, there is no difficulty. Only on the supposition that the Magisterium is speaking of the act as a natural kind, not as a moral act, would there be a difference, whereas the revisionist is including deliberate intention when he speaks of the object of the moral act. But neither thinks the physical act as such is the moral act, pace the revisionist, therefore the difficulty, if there is one, lies elsewhere.

Where it lies is in the desire of the revisionist to treat an ulterior end as if it were a proximate end and thus part of the object of the act. What makes the solitary sex act immoral, according to Father McCormick, is self-pleasuring. Deliberately to engage in it in order to provide sperm for testing is, he contends, a different kind of moral act, having a different object. To this, Russell Hittinger objects that this looks like "self-pleasuring + the further end or aim of obtaining sperm to be tested". And then the act that has been judged wrong, self-pleasuring, is taken to be okay because of this further intention. Father McCormick rejoins that there is not any act to have a further end, that a solitary sex act becomes a morally okay act when it is deliberately engaged in to obtain sperm for testing. "The intention makes the act what it is. . . ."[3] He suggests that we use "motive" for the further or ulterior ends for which we act and reserve "intention" for the object of the act.

The difficulty with this is that it makes defining almsgiving independently of the further intention difficult. To intend to give alms is deliberately to give money or other goods to another who is poor; what is given must be the giver's to give. This is sufficient as an object of a human act. It would be contrasted with my intending to give your money without your consent to the poor. So there is almsgiving and, say, an illicit transfer of goods. These are objects, aims, or intentions of contrasting human or moral acts. A further intention or aim of the act—what McCormick calls its motive—might vitiate an act. For example, almsgiving is a good thing to do, but to do it with an eye to garnering praise vitiates it. On the other hand, a good aim, intention, or motive, say, helping the poor, cannot redeem an act of theft, however much sympathy you might feel for Robin Hood. Stealing from the rich remains stealing, whatever its motive.

Father McCormick's problem would seem to be this. He assumes that there is an intention in self-pleasuring that makes the action bad, but it is difficult for critics like Hittinger to see what that might be. What if it is said that self-pleasuring for relief of tension is the object of the act and to speak of mere self-pleasuring is biologism or physicalism? Could the intention of "relief from tension" characterize the act in the same way that "for sperm testing" does? It is this sliding from the act done to the motive that prompts Hittinger's charge that just shifting attention is taken to constitute the moral properties of the act. Is self-pleasuring a kind of moral act, as almsgiving is, with relief from tension—or sperm testing—a further end like vainglory? Despite disclaimers, Father McCormick seems to confuse a single human act that is made up of a distinguishable act relating to another distinguishable act as means to end, and unified in that way, from the way in which the distinguishable components could be single human acts. To give alms for the sake of vainglory is a unified action comprising almsgiving, which is morally describable as such and the further motive of vanity. What would otherwise be a good moral action, almsgiving, is vitiated because of this motive. Until Father McCormick can give us the aim or end or intent that renders self-pleasuring morally wrong, we will not know how to exclude such motives as relief of tension from the object of the act. Is not the revised sense of "object" a sense of the term which would only apply to the means (almsgiving) and end (vainglory) of the *complex* act?

This discussion can and must go on. It concerns, as *Veritatis Splendor* makes clear, what is meant by the object of the human act. What is somewhat disingenuous about Father McCormick's example is that obtaining sperm for testing has not been the kind of solitary sex act that revisionist theologians have sanctioned. Rather, what one has heard again and again is that self-pleasuring, in Father McCormick's phrase, is morally okay. One has heard that masturbation, fornication, adultery, and homosexual acts can be morally justified. The Holy Father, defending traditional Christian morality, has pointed out that such acts are intrinsically wrong because of their objects.

In the circumstances, given the unclarity in the positions of the revisionists, taken singly and collectively, it is unseemly on their part to chide the Holy Father in the manner of one speaking to a dull student. The fact is that the position of *Veritatis Splendor* is crystal clear and that of the revisionists, as one can see in the review article by Father McCormick, needs work. Over the past twenty-five years, Catholic moralists have been saying that acts that have always been regarded as intrinsically evil are somehow morally okay, at least at times. To say that one does not allow that an intrinsically evil act may be done because he has some new and obscure notion of what constitutes the object of the act is a disingenuous way to escape the sting of the encyclical's condemnation.

Most of the moral matters under discussion in the encyclical are susceptible of resolution on a purely natural or philosophical basis. But we live in times when ears have become deaf to the truths of natural morality. The situation has been complicated by the fact that voices within the Church have adopted positions more in accord with the circumambient secularism than with the Christian tradition. Hence the need for *Veritatis Splendor*. Now is the time for Catholic scholars to come to the defense of natural and Christian morality. Now is the time for Catholic scholars to thank God for the Magisterium and for Pope John Paul II.

NOTES

1 *Theological Studies* 55 (1994): 481–506.
2 Ibid., 494.
3 Ibid., 495.

RUSSELL HITTINGER

AQUINAS AND THE RULE OF LAW

I

The renowned English legal philosopher Herbert Hart maintained that "the introduction into society of rules enabling legislators to change and add to the rules of duty, and judges to determine when the rules of duty have been broken, is a step forward as important to society as the invention of the wheel."[1] For Hart, when a society moves from having rules to having rules governing the making of rules, that society can be said to move from a pre-legal to a legal condition. It is only with the introduction of the idea of a rule of law that law itself becomes available to society, for until there is a rule of law, there is no basis for picking out, from among the myriad of commands, those commands that are truly and validly legal. Perhaps historians can tell us when and where this momentous evolution took place. But that there could be a society totally bereft of at least the rudimentary practices of a rule of law does strain the imagination.

As a thought experiment, we might imagine a society in which whoever exercises authority makes no reference to the source of his authority; or, what is the same thing, imagine a society in which the people exhibit no interest whatsoever in how political authority is transmitted between generations. Imagine a society in which the chieftain gives commands ad hoc, out of the saddle, as it were ("bring me the horse!"), but fails to distinguish between these pell-mell commands and laws that are meant to apply generally and to persist over time ("whosoever fails to bring the horse shall die"). Imagine a society so primitive as to have discovered no need to resolve disputes in reference to independently existing standards and procedures—or a society that approves the practice of an individual being the judge in his own case.

Perhaps there are, or have been, such societies. The point is that it is hard to imagine organized social life without at least the rudiments of the rule of law. The Bible reports that the rule of law was there at the very beginning. For we recall that in the second chapter of Genesis, the Lord God gave a law: "You may eat freely of every tree of the garden; but of the tree of the knowledge of good and evil you shall not eat, for in the day that you eat of it you shall die" (Gen 2:17). Except for the Gnostics, no one ever pretended that this injunction was a dietary prescription. If it did not concern the diet of our first parents, then what exactly was forbidden? The Church Fathers unanimously interpreted this injunction to be chiefly jurisdictional in nature. God retains jurisdiction over the primary measures of moral good and evil; the human mind receives, but does not make, the first norms of justice. Indeed, this itself is the first rule of justice and the root of the natural law. Tertullian characterized the injunction "as the womb of all the precepts of God"—a "law unwritten, which was habitually understood naturally".[2] All commands are based, originally and ultimately, in a scheme by which men participate in divine governance. Our first parents were given a gift of participation, not a grant of plenary power. Hence, the injunction in Gen 2:17 forbids men from usurping God's jurisdiction. In other words, the first law established a rule of law. The rule of law was not an artifact like the wheel; and if a particular society "invented" a rule of law, it was only a reinvention or a recovery of a principle given in the natural commonwealth at creation.

And so, farther on in Genesis, we read that, after slaying Abel, Cain cried out "whoever finds me will slay me." And the Lord said, "Not so! If anyone slays Cain, vengeance will be taken on him sevenfold" (Gen 4:15f.). God placed a mark on Cain, signifying that private parties do not have authority to exact punishments, even if the deed is a capital offense. Those who would (simply on their own recognizance) kill Cain are doing the same thing that Cain did and, indeed, the same thing that Cain's parents did: namely, they are helping themselves to authority. According to the Church Fathers, the sin of our first parents and the subsequent unraveling of society in the lives of their children were the result of a violation of the rule of law. What we see in Genesis is a legal order coming apart—though, to be sure, it was not a legal order overseen by blokes in powdered wigs.

As a theologian, Saint Thomas Aquinas, too, subscribed to the authority of the scriptural story. There was not morality, then laws, and then a rule of law. The entailment runs in the opposite direction. In creating, God established sovereignty over creatures; he gave a rule of recognition for his jurisdictional authority; and this rule is nothing other than the primordial norm of justice, instilled in the human mind without any need of written arts. It is called the natural law. After sin, the structure was given once again at Sinai, though this time in the form of writing. At Sinai, God did not merely issue a set of commandments; rather, he promulgated a system of injunctions, beginning with, "I am the Lord thy God." Saint Thomas insisted that every precept of the Decalogue carries the note of God's jurisdictional authority.[3] The fourth commandment, enjoining obedience to parents, refers also to the obligation to obey delegated authority; the fifth commandment, says Saint Thomas, essentially forbids us to kill on our own authority; the sixth commandment, he argues, refers back to Genesis, where God himself instituted matrimony.

Though he wrote on the subject of law primarily in the office of a theologian, Saint Thomas had much to say about law and about the theme of the rule of law. Not all of it is a matter of scriptural exegesis. For Thomas, the human art of providing institutions for a rule of law is art imitating the activities of nature, albeit created nature. By nature, human beings do something more than merely give commands, which are called "laws"; they also create, by custom and by deliberate art, institutional contexts for laws.

What I shall do in this paper is to focus upon a few of the most interesting things that Thomas had to say about this subject. First, I shall make some general comments about how, for Saint Thomas, the very idea of law implicitly contains the idea of a rule of law. Second, I shall discuss why limited government under the rule of law is rooted in a metaphysic of art imitating nature. Finally, I shall take up a disputed subject of our own day and see what Saint Thomas had to say about it: namely, whether laws ought to be made by judges.

II

Most everyone, I suppose, is familiar with Thomas' famous definition of law: "*It is nothing else than an ordinance of reason for the common good, made by him who has care of the community, and promulgated.*"[4] According to this definition, law is not mere force; it is not a matter of physical but moral necessity. It rather imparts some kind of necessity in the order of practical reason, concerning things to be done. Concerning which things to be done? Those things ordered to a common good. Accordingly, law is not just any kind of morally legitimate command. One says to his child, "you must take a shower and go to bed." Yet it would be odd to think that one thereby issues a curfew for all of the children in the neighborhood. Law requires credentials of authority—and not just domestic authority, but authority to bind and direct a political multitude.

Precisely because law directs a multitude, it can be distinguished from counsels and admonitions. Counsels and admonitions can guide an individual person. We say, for example, you ought to do it this way, not that way; we do not pretend, however, that our direction necessarily applies beyond this single act, *hic et nunc*; or beyond the individual to whom we give counsel. Think of the case of a Brother Placid, who tells the Abbot that every time he goes to the cellar to fetch a bottle of wine, he is harassed by a demon who tempts him to consume the entire bottle. The Abbot gives the matter some thought and advises Brother Placid: The next time you go to the cellar, say a Pater Noster and keep your mouth shut until you get to the refectory. Now, the Abbot does indeed give direction, and the monk would be wrong to ignore it, but the Abbot does not make, or for that matter apply, a law. Even if the Abbot should say that the monk must always follow this procedure, the Abbot does not thereby govern the monastery; rather, he only intends to govern Brother Placid.

Ordinarily, when we reason practically, we try to achieve adequation to the singular circumstance. But when we reason about matters of law, we usually try to achieve what might be called adequate generality.[5] As he says in the *Summa*: "lex est praeceptum commune", law is a general precept.[6] To be sure, in addition to there being general precepts, some laws might also be universal in nature, in the sense that what is enjoined or forbidden is, in the very nature of the thing, a duty, for example. "Thou shall not murder." Other laws bind human action, not necessarily because of the nature of the act enjoined or forbidden, but because an authority has reached a determination, for example: Give an accounting of your taxes no later than April 15.

Whether it be a general and universal principle of conduct, or whether it be a general standing precept, what makes a law different from other dictates of practical reason is the direction of human conduct by means of a *leges communes*. "Law would be of no use", Thomas writes, "if it did not extend farther than to one single act. The decrees of the prudent are made for the purpose of directing individual actions, whereas law is a general precept."[7] Yves Simon has captured the issue rather nicely: "The principle of government by law is subject to such precarious conditions that, if it were not constantly reasserted, it soon would be destroyed by the opposite and complementary principle, viz. that of adequacy to contingent, changing, and unique circumstances."[8]

I understand Simon to be saying that if there were no political good to be accomplished, then human beings would only have to exercise the virtue of right reason on a case by case basis. There would be no need for *leges communes*. Simon is surely correct. Whether we are fixing furnaces or educating children or doing the right thing by our spouses and friends, the human mind naturally gravitates toward achieving rightness in the specific case. This is why all of us have experienced, at one time or another, the aggravating problem of legalism, when laws try to interrupt or supplant our natural gravitation to contingent singulars. But, by nature man has social and political ends, and therefore there is need for governance by laws. As Simon remarked, without law, these social ends can be destroyed by our habits of individual prudence. In fact, in the *Summa*, Saint Thomas speculated that even in the state of innocence, where there is no need of criminal law, there would still be need of general standing precepts. We can imagine a society of motorists in the state of innocence; every motorist is perfectly virtuous and able to adapt his vehicle to the conditions of the road; but even so, there would be need for a general standing law directing the multitude to drive on the right hand side of the road.[9]

For Saint Thomas, law is a moral exercise. It directs rational agents in what should be done in the way of action. But it is a distinctive kind of moral exercise. Jurisprudence requires something more than moral virtue; it also requires virtues we associate with art. In his commentary on the *Ethics*, Thomas compares rulers imposing laws in civic matters to architects regarding things to be built—"sicut architectores in artificialibus."[10] Framing, enforcing, and adjudicating *leges communes* is no easy matter. Once an authority starts to supply laws, he will find that the community needs something more than a bunch of laws that are morally worthy, one by one; it also needs a system of law, by which I mean laws that do not conflict with one another; laws regulating how conflicts shall be resolved; and laws stipulating how bad or inefficient laws can be changed. Lawgivers, law-enforcers, and law-adjudicators will themselves need some direction.

III

Most everyone will admit that it is useful to have rules governing those who make and administrate laws. Saint Thomas suggests that rules of law are more than merely useful. In his commentary on Aristotle's *Politics*, he writes: "When a man has sole and absolute power over everything, his rule is said to be regal. When, on the other hand, he rules in accord with the disciplined instructions [*sermones disciplinales*], that is, in accordance with laws laid down by the discipline of politics, his rule is political. It is as though he were part ruler, namely, as regards the things that come under his power, and part subject, as regards the things in which he is subject to the law."[11] Where there are no *sermones disciplinales*—no rules of law, as it were there is no discipline of politics.

In the West, unqualified regal rule was rejected in principle, if not always in practice. The feudal system, for example, distributed the rights and responsibilities of governance to many minds and to many sources of decision making. The sovereign was limited from above, by God, and limited from below, by *sermones disciplinales*, consisting of customs, private law, common law, and a myriad of civil organizations, from guilds to universities. After 1140, the Church herself was governed in the external forum by a code of canon law that limited and determined her legal procedures.[12] It is true that medieval Christian thinkers, including Saint Thomas, praised monarchy as the most perfect principle; but the most perfect principle is not necessarily the most perfect institution.

As we mentioned earlier, Saint Thomas held that the operations of art imitate the operations of nature. In the prologue to his commentary on Aristotle's *Politics*, he notes that "if art were to make natural things, it would operate in the same way as nature, and, conversely, if nature were to produce artifacts, it would make them the way art does."[13] When human beings create a system of law, what is being imitated? It is worth pausing for a moment to consider this point more carefully.

In the first place, we imitate the divine manner of governing a multitude. In his letter to the King of Cyprus, Thomas urged the king to take as his pattern the "regime of nature" [*a forma regiminis naturalis*], and the "example of the creation of the world" [*ab exemplo institutionis mundi*].[14] From the "regime of nature", we see parts disposed to a whole and means directed to ends. Any sort of complex whole requires a principle of unity. In this sense, monarchy is the most perfect principle.

But the art of governance does not just take its pattern from the principle of unity. We also see in nature one thing perfecting another and that thing, in turn, perfecting yet another. "God wished to produce his works in likeness to himself, as far as possible, in order that they might be perfect and that he might be known through them. Hence, that he might be portrayed in his works, not only according to what he is in himself but also according as he acts on others, he laid this natural law on all things, that last things should be reduced and perfected by middle things, and middle things by the first, as Dionysius says."[15] Interestingly, here the phrase natural law is not used to designate any particular law; rather, it is used in reference to the lawfulness of a system—namely, a system in which the whole is brought to perfection by means of the parts perfecting one another. It is a scheme of participation.[16] The art of politics and law, therefore, requires not only a principle of unity (represented in the monarchical office) but also a principle of multiplicity and hierarchy. The word *politia*, Saint Thomas observes, is simply a generic name for a government administered by many.[17]

A plan of governance, he says in the *Summa Theologiae*, always requires a provision for secondary governors, just as the plan of

AQUINAS AND THE RULE OF LAW 107

an architect is imparted to subordinate craftsmen, who take the general rules and apply them—perhaps even making additional rules of their own.[18] Clearly, laws issued from "command central", as it were, are not enough for the perfection of a project as simple as building a house, much less a project as complex as a political society. This is why Saint Thomas, along with virtually all legal theorists prior to Bentham, held that custom is a kind of law. For custom is a quasi-natural way by which the parts of the polity perfect one another; custom reflects an order achieved through reciprocities rather than through the exercise of raw, unmediated legislative power. "[C]ustom", Thomas insisted, "has the force of a law, abolishes law, and is the interpreter of law."[19]

Although monarchy might be the most perfect principle, the most perfect polity is the mixed regime. The merits of the mixed regime are confirmed not only by the authority of Aristotle but in the Pentateuch, especially Deuteronomy. God, the Creator of the natural commonwealth, established a mixed regime. Again, what is better to imitate than the divine art itself? Saint Thomas writes:

> Accordingly, the best form of government is in a state or kingdom, wherein one, who is especially qualified, is given the power to preside over all, while under him are other governors having special qualifications; and yet a government of this kind is shared by all, both because all are eligible to govern and because the rulers are chosen by all. This is the best form of polity, being partly kingship, since there is one at the head of all; partly aristocracy, insofar as a number of persons are set in authority; partly democracy, that is, government by the people, insofar as the rulers can be chosen from the people, and as it belongs to the people to choose their rulers. Such was the form of government established by the divine law.[20]

The art of law imitates the activities of nature in yet another respect—one that is very important. From experience, we know that no human mind is a ruling-rule. In order to make rules, we first need to receive one. Therefore, when a plan of government is established, reason dictates that there is needed something in addition to the principles of unity and distribution. We also need some institutional recognition that the human sovereign is not a *mensura prima*. Saint Augustine said: "Only God can be happy by his own power with no one ruling."[21] Augustine's maxim, applied to human government, means that whoever rules must himself be ruled.

By nature, the finite human mind is not a ruling-rule but a ruled-rule; it is fitting that in the art of politics whoever makes laws for the common good should himself be subjected to laws. Saint Thomas said that human reason "is not of itself the rule of things, but the principles impressed on it by nature are general rules and measures of all things relating to human conduct."[22] Human reason, of course, can make rules; but it does so only if it first receives a rule. No human being makes rules or laws from scratch, because no human mind is a rule or law unto itself. For God, nature and law are the same; but for the creature, there is no such thing, strictly speaking, as autonomy.[23] "Man does not make the law for himself," Thomas explains, "but through the act of his knowledge, by which he knows a law made by someone else, he is bound to fulfill the law."[24]

No doubt, the idea of the rule of law reflects certain practical, let us even say pragmatic, exigencies of social and political life. The institutional details of a rule of law, of course, vary from culture to culture. It needs to be emphasized, however, that the idea of a rule of law does not simply arise from certain accidental features of the human condition; it is not a mere convenience, artfully instituted for the purpose of curbing our passions and rectifying our ignorance. The need for a rule of law is endemic to the natural condition of man. When we hear it said that we ought to have a government of law rather than of men, the adage bespeaks a truth about human nature. Whoever rules must first receive a rule, which is only another way of saying that no one is a rule unto himself. Where the absolutely first rule comes from is a subject of philosophical, if not theological, investigation. Yet in ordinary experience, we understand that no human mind is a law unto itself.

Having said this, it is necessary to say that political and legal arts can play a defensive role. Once again, I quote from Thomas' letter to the King of Cyprus: "Then, once the king is established, the government of the kingdom must be so arranged that opportunity to tyrannize is removed. At the same time his power should be so tempered that he cannot easily fall into tyranny."[25] What does it mean to temper the power of the king? Does it mean that the king, given an absolute power to govern, must govern according to the dictates of morality and justice? Are we only saying that the king must make laws in such a way that he protects the innocent and provides for the common good? Not quite. When Saint Thomas insists that the government must be "so arranged" that the opportunity to tyrannize is "removed", he means that the king must be brought under a rule of law. Or, to put it in another way, a government must opt for political rather than regal rule. And to opt for political rule means that the sovereign must have *sermones disciplinales*.[26]

Thus far, I have not addressed any particular institution of the rule of law. I have tried to locate the theme within some general principles discussed by Saint Thomas. Before I move on to a particular legal institution, it would be good to summarize these general principles. First, the practice of the rule of law is ultimately rooted in the nature of the human mind. Precisely because the human mind is not, absolutely speaking, a measuring-measure, it has need of law. And this need applies not only to those who are governed but also to those who govern. Second, the practice of the rule of law stems from an implication of the first principle: because the human mind is not a ruling-rule, Saint Thomas rejects the project of regal rule. Monarchical rule, within a mixed government—yes; but regal rule, purely and simply—no. Not even God governs by regal rule. For creatures are permitted to participate in divine governance and thereby play some role in directing and perfecting one another. This participation is not vouchsafed only to the human prince. When those who govern are themselves placed under law, we are not merely bowing to prudence; regal rule is to be rejected not merely because it is inconvenient but because it is *contra naturam*. Third, when human art imitates the activities of nature, it is necessary not only to make laws in order to dispose the parts to the common good; it is also necessary to frame institutions that protect the rule of law. In this respect, we can quote James Madison, who wrote in *Federalist Papers*, no. 51: "In framing a government which is to be administered by men over men, the great difficulty lies in this; you must first enable the government to control the governed; and in the next place oblige it to control itself." Now the way these institutions are framed depends in considerable part upon prudence.

IV

As should be clear by now, Saint Thomas rejects any institution of raw, legislative power. When we think of such power, we usually think of a dictator like Mussolini. Interestingly, Saint Thomas actually has us consider a more beguiling example of the temptation toward regal rather than political rule. Without doubt, Thomas had much to say about kings becoming tyrants. But he also warned about the danger of rule by judges. In this respect, his political theory is quite relevant to our own polity, which seems to be governed by a judicial oligarchy.

The issue of rule by judges, in fact, surfaces in the *Summa Theologiae*, in the first article of the first question devoted to human law. The question is whether "it was useful for laws to be framed by men." In one of the objections, it is pointed out that, as Aristotle said, animate justice, which proceeds from the virtue and character of the wise man, is more reliable than the lifeless justice represented in written laws. Rather than having a legislator frame general standing laws, why not find a virtuous Judge Wapner, as it were, to make law on a case by case basis?

Saint Thomas responds:

> It should be said that, as the Philosopher says in I *Rhet.*, "it is better that all things be regulated by law than left to be decided by judges."[27] And this for three reasons. First, because it is easier to find a few wise men competent to frame right laws than to find the many who would be necessary to judge aright of each single case. Second, because those who make laws consider long beforehand what laws to make, whereas judgment on each single case has to be pronounced as soon as it arises. It is easier for man to see what is right by taking many instances into consideration than by considering one solitary fact. Third, because lawgivers judge in the abstract and of future events, whereas those who sit in judgment judge of things present, toward which they are affected by love, hatred, or some kind of cupidity, and hence their judgment is perverted. Since, then, the animated justice of the judge is not found in every man, and since it can be deflected, it was necessary, whenever possible, for the law to determine how to judge and for very few matters to be left to the decision of men.[28]

In this passage, Saint Thomas is making two points. First, a system of law is not the same thing as a collection of judgments. What is reasonable in a single case is not necessarily adequate for governing a political community in a multitude of cases. Judge-made law—or, to put it in another way, law that is merely a codification of judicial decisions—is not likely to achieve what we earlier called adequate generality. The fact that this or that decision is just (for example, that this student does not have to meet a language requirement) does not mean that the ruling would be just if applied to others. Thus, to avoid injustice, each and every law would have to be the law of the individual case. We would, in effect, have a polity without statutes; in short, we would not have anything resembling a human polity.

Second, Saint Thomas points out that allowing judges to make law in the single case is not only to invite failure in the order of legal art but to invite corruption. We need general, standing laws (preferably written) for two purposes: (1) in order to have laws capable of prospectively directing the entire community, and (2) in order to set a rule for the mind of the judge. The law, he says, ought to determine how the judge judges; judges should not determine the law, at least not in any direct fashion.

In regard to the danger of rule by judges, Thomas recalls the last sentence of the Book of Judges: "In those days there was no king in Israel: every man did what was good in his own eyes (Jg 21:25)."[29] Sound familiar? Imagine a political society governed by so many judicial Jimmy Carters; a sort of sincere cracker-barrel justice, according to which every man does what is good "in his own eyes". When it pertains to private matters, everyone must, of course, do what is good "in his own eyes". The question, however, is whether judges should judge according to what seems good. Saint Thomas says No. The jurisdiction of the judge should be limited; he must be made to judge and to fashion remedies according to the written law.

It might be objected that there exist certain natural norms of justice, to which the conscience of every rightly formed mind has access. These norms of justice do not need the approval of human legal institutions. Indeed, precisely because these norms are not made by human agents, they stand in judgment of human laws and institutions. Now, it hardly needs to be said that Saint Thomas believed in the existence of a natural law, which is nothing else than that part of the eternal law that men know naturally. But the question before us is not whether there exists a natural law; rather, the question concerns the authority of men to make judgments that bind other men. Of course, the natural law prohibits theft. But this dictate of natural justice still leaves much to be determined: for example, the manner in which this evil is to be policed or tolerated; who should resolve disputes over it; how and when penalties ought to be assigned. The natural law leaves indeterminate who and how the natural law is to be enforced.

The office of judge is a quasi-natural office; any minimally developed polity will provide for someone to make judgments in the name of the entire community. But no one holds the office by natural right. (Incidentally, unlike John Locke, who famously asserted that by natural right, every person is judge and executor of the natural law, Saint Thomas held that authority is always held by political arrangement—whether by God, by other men, or by both. Authority is naturally vested in the body politic, but no person has a natural right to the office of judge. So, whereas Locke argued that men enter into civil society in order to overcome the inconvenience of exercising their natural rights, Saint Thomas contended that men are political from the outset and that whatever inconveniences political offices are meant to correct, they certainly do not correct a natural right to exercise the office of judgment. In short, the existence of natural law does not mean that anyone has a natural right to be the public judge of that law.)

When legislators commit laws to writing, they bind judges to resolve disputes about the law according to what was laid down in writing. The legislator has the first authority to make law in accordance with what is deemed to be the law of nature. In a strikingly interesting passage in the *Summa*, Saint Thomas maintains that the judge who usurps the authority of the legislator violates both the positive and natural laws.

> It should be said that . . . judgment is nothing else but a decision or determination [*definitio vel determinatio*] of what is just. Now a thing becomes just in two ways: first, by the very nature of the case [*ex ipsa natura rei*], and this is called the natural right [*ius naturale*]; second, by some agreement between men [*ex quodam condicto inter homines*], and this is called positive right [*ius positivum*]. . . . Now laws are written for the purpose of manifesting both these rights, but in different ways. For the written law does indeed contain natural right, but it does not establish it, for the latter derives its force, not from the law, but from

nature; whereas the written law both contains positive right and establishes it by giving it force of authority. Hence it is necessary to judge according to the written law, else judgment would fall short either of the natural or of the positive right.[30]

Recall what we said earlier. According to Saint Thomas, God does not only govern men in an immediate fashion—let us say, by instilling the natural law in every human mind; he also governs through a political order in which one subordinate agent perfects another. And this is precisely what we are doing when we insist that the judge has authority to declare what is binding upon the parties in the case only if the judge himself is directed by certain *sermones disciplinales*. When the judge lays down the decision, relying upon no directives except his own personal sense of what is right, that judge has claimed regal as against political rule. Coincidentally, the judge might arrive at a just decision; but he does not arrive at the decision justly. This is why Saint Thomas maintains that such a judgment falls short of both the natural and the legal standards of justice.

"In matters touching his own person," Thomas writes, "a man must form his conscience from his own knowledge, but in matters concerning the public authority, he must form his conscience in accordance with the knowledge attainable in the public judicial procedure."[31] Suppose that the judge is morally certain that witnesses have lied, rendering a morally innocent defendant vulnerable to execution. This would be a concrete test for Thomas' understanding of the morality of offices. Where is the judge's duty? Does it consist primarily in his moral judgment about the status of the defendant, or does it consist primarily in his office determined by *sermones disciplinales*? Saint Thomas answers:

> If the judge knows that a man who has been convicted by false witnesses is innocent, he must, like Daniel, examine the witnesses with great care, so as to find a motive for acquitting the innocent: but if he cannot do this, he should remit him for judgment by a higher tribunal. If even this is impossible, he does not sin if he pronounce sentence in accordance with the evidence,

for it is not he who puts the innocent man to death, but they who stated him to be guilty.[32]

Admittedly, this would be the extreme case testing the rule of law; but Saint Thomas makes his point clearly and forcefully. Just as the legislator has a duty to make law for the common good, so, too, whoever has authority to adjudicate the law has a superordinate duty to the body politic. His first duty is to the rule of law. Since no one has a natural right to judge, but rather receives that authority from the community, a judge who ignores the bounds fixed by the positive law exceeds his authority. He acts, as the lawyers say, *ultra vires*. And to act *ultra vires* is nothing other than to make or impose a law without authority to do so; this is a violation of the natural law.

In an 1853 circuit case, Justice John McClean made the following observation about the limits on judicial authority.

> It is for the people, who are sovereign, and their representatives, in making constitutions and the enactment of laws, to consider the laws of nature, and the immutable principles of right. This is a field which judges cannot explore. . . . They look to the law, and to the law only. A disregard of this by the judicial powers, would undermine and overturn the social compact.[33]

Even giving allowance for the fact that the case concerned judicial obligation to apply the fugitive slave clause (art. 4, §2), I do not think that Saint Thomas would disagree with Justice McClean's understanding of the principle that binds the judge. Unlike Superman or Jimmy Carter, judges are not free-roving instruments of justice. Along with Justice McClean, Thomas holds that obedience to the rule of law is a superordinate moral duty for a public officer. The judge's obedience to the limits imposed by the political order is itself a dictate of the natural law.

But, it must be asked, what if the written law is deficient? Judges, Saint Thomas argued, are certainly obligated to give equity; that is, to assist the general law in reaching the contingent details of the particular case at hand. No written law is perfect.

Whenever a law is written down, someone will need to interpret it. Saint Thomas understood that judges must interpret
the law—it is part of the art of judging to fashion remedies
skillfully, including remedies that are only implicitly contained
in the written law. Indeed, a judge who refuses to give equity,
through interpreting the written law, is disobedient to the will
of the legislator. But when the judge gives equity, Thomas
adds, he does not pass judgment on the law itself; rather, he
remains obedient to the law by stretching the letter of the law
in order to make it effective in the case.[34] Equity is not an act
of judicial law making.

Hence, when the judge gives equity, he perfects the intention of the lawgiver—provided, of course, that he does not
usurp authority. To be sure, in giving equity, judges can im-
pede the rule of law. It could happen that a polity ends up
with two tracks of law: the written statutes and a set of what
Saint Thomas calls judicial *sententialia*. One gets one kind of
justice from the trial court and yet another kind of justice
from the court of equity. If this two-tiered justice were not
brought under some control, the legal system would become
dysfunctional. By the way, this is why our framers, in article 3, section 2 of the Constitution, did away with independent
courts of equity; for they remembered the arbitrary way that
the Crown administered courts of equity in the colonies. Go
back and read the Declaration of Independence, where Mr. Jef-
ferson complains not only about violations of natural rights but
also about violations of colonial legislatures by the courts.[35] It is
also worth bearing in mind that four of the first eight amend-
ments deal with limits on the federal judiciary. They had a
living memory of mischief making by royal courts. As John
Randolph remarked, I seem to recall that the Book of Judges
was followed by the Book of Kings.

But, what if the law is not merely deficient but corrupt?
Morally speaking, a judge is under no obligation to apply a
corrupt law. He can recuse himself from the case, or he can
resign his office. The question, however, is whether the judge

can change the law. Notice, it is one thing to refuse to apply a law; it is quite another thing to change a law, in such a way that the judge makes a new law. It is never permissible to make or enforce laws that one has no authority to make or enforce. Thomas observes that, "even as it would be unjust for one man to force another to observe a law that was not approved by public authority, so too it is unjust if a man compels another to submit to a judgment that is pronounced by other than the public authority."[36] Thus, we could say that a judge in the Third Reich has a moral duty to thwart the injustice, within the scope of means provided to him as a public officer; if this fails, he could have a moral duty to resign from the bar. Yet the judge has no authority vested in his own person to make, emend, or change German law. Even in the case of justifiable resistance against a tyrant, Thomas remained quite insistent that the resistance must be "undertaken, not through the private presumption of a few, but rather by public authority".[37] No doubt, what it means to resist the tyrant on the approval of public authority is pretty vague. Yet, even in our own revolution, royal governance was overthrown by men who represented legislatures. True enough, they cited the law of nature; nevertheless, it was cited and applied on the basis of something more than their private recognizance. At least for Saint Thomas, resistance or revolution must be done according to a rule of law.

V

To conclude and summarize, the idea of the rule of law in Saint Thomas is based upon three principles.

First, it is rooted in the truth that the human mind is not a measuring-measure. In matters of law, there is no such thing as autonomy—at least not for the finite mind. "What [God] does according to his will, he does justly: as we do justly what we do according to law. But whereas law comes to us from some higher power, God is a law unto himself."[38] That the human mind must be governed by law is natural; it is not merely the result of sin. Second, the idea of a rule of law is rooted in the nature of political order. In political rule, the parts perfect one another. Whether we consider the divine governance of the cosmos or the harmonious functions of the human body, we see that nature contains not only a principle of unity but also a principle of distributive justice (what the whole owes to the parts). This principle cannot be embodied in regal rule. For in regal rule, the sovereign simply issues commands and backs them up with coercive sanctions. For Saint Thomas, this is not a rule of law, because it is not political rule. Third, there is need for what might be called a defensive principle. Given the weakness and corruptibility of the human will, it is necessary to place institutional limits upon those who govern. With legal and political officials, we do not want merely to cite the Augustinian dictum: "Love God and do what you will." Rather, we want their powers to be exercised within an institutional system of laws. It should be emphasized that the first two principles are entirely positive and natural. They are not essentially pragmatic. The last one is, of course, pragmatic.

As a concluding thought experiment, we can ask ourselves what would become of a legal culture if it lost its sense of the first two principles. Suppose a legal culture comes to believe that the human mind is a measuring-measure? Take, for example, the dictum in *Planned Parenthood v Casey* (1992): "At the heart of liberty is the right to define one's own concept of existence, of meaning, of the universe, and of the mystery of human life. Beliefs about these matters could not define the attributes of personhood were they formed under compulsion of the State."

What would happen to the rule of law if people actually believed this dictum? Since all positive law limits the ways in which human persons define themselves, it would seem to follow that individuals, by nature, have a right of immunity from positive law, which is another way of saying that individuals have an immunity from politics. And if there are natural rights to be immune from politics, why not secure these rights by regal rule? And if laws are unnatural fences upon human liberty, how can there be any natural limits to the power of the human sovereign? I recommend these thoughts for your further reflection. To pursue them here would be another paper.

NOTES

¹ H. L. A. Hart, *The Concept of Law* (Oxford: Clarendon Press, 1961), p. 41.

² *Adv. Judaeos*, cap. 2 (PL 2–2, 599, 600), "quasi matrix omnium praeceptorum Dei . . . non scriptam, quae naturaliter intelligebatur."

³ *ST* I–II, 100, 8. See also *Collationes in Decem Praeceptis*.

⁴ *ST* I–II, 90, 4.

⁵ As Saint Thomas said in his commentary on the *Ethics*, it is one thing to have a science of morals; it is quite another thing to have a science of legislation (*In X Eth.*, lectio 14, no. 2137).

⁶ *ST* I–II, 96, 1 ad 2.

⁷ *ST* I–II, 92, 2.

⁸ Yves Simon, *The Tradition of Natural Law*, intro. Russell Hittinger (New York: Fordham University Press, 1992), p. 84.

⁹ "Such a kind of mastership would have existed in the state of innocence between man and man, for two reasons. First, because man is naturally a social being, and so in the state of innocence he would have led a social life. Now a social life cannot exist among a number of people unless under the presidency of one to look after the common good; for many, as such, seek many things, whereas one attends only to one. Wherefore the Philosopher says, in the beginning of the *Politics*, that wherever many things are directed to one, we shall always find one at the head directing them" (*ST* I, 96, 4).

¹⁰ *In VI Eth.*, lectio 7, no. 1197.

¹¹ *In I Pol.*, lectio 1, no. 13.

¹² As a token of the high regard afforded the rule of law in Western culture, Dante, in *Paradiso* X, placed Gratian, the father of canon law, alongside Thomas Aquinas in the fourth heaven, the sphere of the sun.

¹³ *In I Pol.*, prologus, no. 3.

¹⁴ *De Regno*, lib. 2, cap. 1, nos. 93, 99.

¹⁵ *ST*, Supplement, 34, 1: "Hanc legem naturalem imposuit omnibus".

¹⁶ According to which, Thomas defines the natural law: "The light of natural reason whereby we discern what is good and what is evil [*quo discernimus quid sit bonum et quid malum*], and which pertains to the natural law, is nothing else than an imprint on us of the divine light [*impressio luminis divini in nobis*]. It is evident that the natural law is nothing else than the rational creature's participation of the eternal law" (*ST* I–II, 91, 2).

¹⁷ *De Regno* I, 1, 11.

¹⁸ "We observe the same in all those who govern, so that the plan of government is derived by secondary governors from the governor in chief. Thus, the plan of what is to be done in a state flows from the king's command to his

inferior administrators; and again in things of art, the plan of whatever is to be done by art flows from the chief craftsman to the under-craftsmen who work with their hands. Since, then, the eternal law is the plan of government in the supreme governor, all the plans of government in the inferior governors must be derived from the eternal law. But these plans of inferior governors are laws other than the eternal law. Therefore, all laws, insofar as they partake of right reason, are derived from the eternal law. On account of this, Augustine states in *De Lib. Arbit.* I, that 'in temporal law there is nothing just and lawful, but what man has drawn from the eternal law'" (*ST* I–II, 93, 3).

[19] *ST* I–II, 97, 3.

[20] *ST* I–II, 105, 1. He continues: "For Moses and his successors governed the people in such a way that each of them was ruler over all, so that there was a kind of kingship. Moreover, seventy-two men were chosen who were elders in virtue; for it is stated in Deuteronomy 1:15: 'I took out of your tribes men wise and honorable and appointed them rulers'; so that there was an element of aristocracy. But it was a democratic government insofar as the rulers were chosen from all the people; for it is stated in Exodus 18:21: 'Provide out of all the people wise men', etc.; and also because the people chose them; thus, it is said in Deuteronomy 1:13: 'Let me have from among you wise men', etc. Consequently, it is evident that the order of political power was well instituted by the law."

[21] *De Genesi contra Manichaeos* II, cap 15, §22.

[22] *ST* I–II, 91, 3 ad 2.

[23] "What he does according to his will he does justly; as we do justly what we do according to law. But whereas law comes to us from some higher power, God is a law unto himself." (*ST* I, 21, 1 ad 2).

[24] *De Veritate*, 17, 3 ad 1.

[25] *De Regno* I, 4, 42.

[26] This system, in fact, is the greatest of all human arts. "Therefore, in order that man might have peace and virtue, it was necessary for laws to be framed. As the Philosopher says in the I *Pol.*, 'as man is the most noble of animals if he be perfect in virtue, so is he the lowest of all if he be severed from law and righteousness. Man can use instruments of reason [*arma rationis*] in order to mitigate his lusts and evil passions, which other animals are unable to do'" (*ST* I–II, 95, 1).

[27] I, 1, 1354a31.

[28] *ST* I–II, 95, 1 ad 2.

[29] *De Regno* I, 4, 34. "Nobody will be able firmly to state: This thing is such and such, when it depends upon the will of another, not to say upon his caprice" (I, 3, 26).

[30] *ST* II–II, 60, 5.

[31] *ST* II–II, 67, 2 ad 4. See also: "It is the duty of a judge to pronounce judgment inasmuch as he exercises public authority, wherefore his judgment

should be based on information acquired by him, not from his knowledge as a private individual, but from what he knows as a public person" (*ST* II–II, 67, 2).

[32] *ST* II–II, 64, 6 ad 3.

[33] *Miller v McQuerry* 17 F 332 (no. 9,583) (Ohio: C.C.D., 1853).

[34] "It would be passing judgment on a law to say that it was not well made [*non esse bene positam*]. But to say that the letter of the law is not to be observed in some particular case is passing judgment, not on the law, but on some particular contingency" (*ST* II–II, 120, 1 ad 2).

[35] "He has erected a multitude of new offices and sent hither swarms of new officers to harass our people and eat out of their substance. . . . He has combined with others to subject us to a jurisdiction foreign to our constitutions & unacknowledged by our laws . . . taking away our charters, abolishing our most valuable laws, and altering fundamentally the form of our governments; suspending our own legislatures, & declaring themselves invested with power to legislate for us in all cases whatsoever. . . . A prince whose character is thus marked by every act which may define a tyrant is unfit to be the ruler of a free people."

[36] *ST* II–II, 60, 6.

[37] *De Regno* I, 6, 48.

[38] *ST* I, 21, 1 ad 2.

Ronald McArthur

SAINT THOMAS AND THE
FORMATION OF THE CATHOLIC MIND

The *Dialogues* of Plato contain so much about so many things
that our difficulties mount when we try to find with exac-
titude the whole intent of any one of them. Many of them
show, however, and some quite forcefully, the importance of
appetite in what looks at first to be the sphere of disinterested
intelligence. Callicles, Gorgias, and Protagoras, to take but a
few prominent examples, show us that desire can play such a
large role in the intellectual life that it is hard to disentangle
the desire that reality be as we want it to be from what we can
hold with evidence about that same reality. Socrates may be
ironic, or simply playful, when he says that after a lifetime of
intellectual activity he knows nothing. His statement nevertheless suggests a salutary truth: wisdom is so difficult to achieve
that only a very few are, finally, wise. While we may rejoice as
Socrates dismantles the arguments of some of his opponents,
and be delighted as they are forced to take ridiculous positions
in upholding their initial assertions, that rejoicing should be
momentary. Who among us would, upon reflection, see himself as so freed from the constraints of his own desires that he
is able to see with perfect equanimity the reality about which
he holds so many opinions?

There are many reasons that explain why wisdom seems to
be reserved for the few, and we all know some of the most
obvious: there are a relatively few who have the opportunity
to give themselves to the life of study; few who study with
persevering effort the very difficult subjects they should learn;

few who pray with constancy for divine help; few who attain the moral purity so conducive to the life of wisdom, that life which Aristotle without revelation thought more divine than human. There is, however, another reason. It is usually overlooked because we tend to minimize its importance. It is this reason I wish now to bring to your attention.

I

Saint Thomas distinguishes two meanings of the Latin word *mos*:

> Sometimes it means custom, in which sense we read (Acts 15:1): *Except you be circumcised after the manner* (morem) *of Moses, you cannot be saved.* Sometimes it means a natural or quasi-natural inclination to do some particular action, in which sense the word is applied to dumb animals. Thus we read (2 Macc 1:2) that *rushing violently upon the enemy, in the manner of lions* (Leonum more), *they slew them:* and the word is used in the same sense (Ps 67:7) when we read: *Who makes man in one manner* (moris) *to dwell in a house.*[1]

When we use the word *mores* in English, we mean, as the dictionary (*The Concise Oxford*) says, "Customs or conventions regarded as essential to or characteristic of a community". And the dictionary then informs us that the word is the plural of the Latin word *mos*, custom. So far, Saint Thomas and the English dictionary agree, but the second meaning of the word, found as well in the Latin dictionary, is worth our attention. While *mos*, as custom, may be best known to us, Saint Thomas yet shows us the connection of the *two* meanings by showing how the *second* meaning, "a natural or quasi-natural inclination to do some particular action", is closely connected to the first. For, as Saint Thomas says, "the other meaning of *mos*, that is, *custom*, is akin to [a natural or quasi-natural inclination], because custom becomes a second nature and produces an inclination similar to a natural one."

Our habits, whether good or evil, become a second nature; they are "quasi-natural inclinations". Custom, in its turn, plays its role in engendering those inclinations. It is because of the importance of custom that Plato would educate the young by accustoming them to only the right music, art, and literature. It is because of the crucial role our habits play that Aristotle claims that only those who are well brought up, and whose acquired inclinations tend toward the good, can study ethics with any profit.

It is relatively easy to see the role of custom in the moral life. Our manner of acting, as adults, and the general culture that surrounds us have an almost decisive influence on the young and incorporate them into a way of life. The family is a clear case; its absence is even clearer. Custom also plays a vital role in the more restricted life we call intellectual. It presents to the intellect, by means of various doctrines and opinions, certain ways of thinking about things and, by so doing, proportions the intellect to those very things. To take just a few examples: (1) We are accustomed to the view that all social life should be understood in terms of *rights*, and hence this is the way we think about politics or society, almost to the exclusion of anything else; (2) we are likewise accustomed to calling the things we desire our *values*, and so, again, our political thought is laced together with talk about values; (3) almost all college students are moral relativists, a view they absorb from their culture; (4) almost all incoming college freshmen will tell you that lines are made up of points, a commonplace they have received from their teachers.

By constantly hearing something said over and over, the intelligence tends to accept it as true, whether or not it *is* true, and the will inclines toward what it hears. Custom, generally, leads us to judge by what we are in the *habit* of hearing. This, again, is true not only in practical matters *but as well in the life of the intellect when it considers things speculatively as well.*

Aristotle gives eloquent witness to this:

The way we receive a lecture depends on our custom; for we expect a lecturer to use the language we are accustomed to, and any other language appears not agreeable but rather unknown and strange because we are not accustomed to it; for the customary is more known. The power of custom is clearly seen in the laws, in which the mythical and childish beliefs prevail over our knowledge of them, because of custom. Some people do not accept statements unless they are expressed mathematically; others unless they are expressed by way of examples; and there are some who demand that a poet be quoted as witness. Again, some demand accuracy in everything, while others are annoyed by it, either because they are not able to follow connections or because they regard it as petty.[2]

Maimonides, in *The Guide of the Perplexed*, gives his own witness of the close tie between custom and habit:

Man has in his nature a love of, and an inclination for, that to which he is habituated. Thus you can see that the people of the desert—not withstanding the disorderliness of their life, the lack of pleasures, and the scarcity of food—dislike the towns, do not hanker after their pleasures, and prefer the bad circumstances to which they are accustomed to good ones to which they are not accustomed. Their souls accordingly would find no repose in living in palaces, in wearing silk clothes, and in the enjoyment of baths, ointments, and perfumes. In a similar way, man has love for, and the wish to defend, opinions to which he is habituated and in which he has been brought up and has a feeling of repulsion for opinions other than those. For this reason also man is blind to the apprehension of the true realities and inclines toward the things to which he is habituated.[3]

Montaigne, in his essay on custom, reaffirms the same power of custom and the intellectual habits it inculcates:

The principal effect of the power of custom is to seize and ensnare us in such a way that it is hardly within our power to get ourselves back out of its grip and return into ourselves to reflect and reason about its ordinances. In truth, because we drink them with our milk from birth, and because the face of the world presents itself in this aspect to our first view, it seems that we are born on condition of following this course. And the common notions that we find in credit around us and infused into our soul by our father's seed, these seem to be the universal and natural ones. Whence it comes to pass that what is off the hinges of custom people believe to be off the hinges of reason.[4]

Saint Augustine, with his own account of his meeting and acquaintance with Saint Ambrose, gives us a luminous example of the role of custom in the life of the intelligence. Trained in rhetoric and a teacher of it and, by the time he came to Milan, skeptical because of his disappointment with the Manicheans, Augustine heard Ambrose preach. Here is his account:

> I attended carefully when he preached to the people, not with the right intention, *but only to judge whether his eloquence was equal to his fame or whether it flowed higher or lower than had been told me.* His words I listened to with the greatest care: his matter I held quite unworthy of attention. I enjoyed the *charm* of his speaking, though for all his learning it was not as *pleasing* or *captivating* as that of Faustus. . . . Thus I did not take great heed to learn what he was saying *but only to hear how he said it.*[5]

Even in the case of a singularly endowed mind, and the mind of one who, for all his sins and corruptions, had by his own assessment diligently sought the truth, there was no escaping the power of the custom that had formed his intellect, a rhetorical formation that is evident in all his writings. Hence he was concerned, not so much with the truth in hearing Saint Ambrose, but with the *mode* of expression, and that according to his own predilections.

Long before his acquaintance with Saint Ambrose, however, Augustine, as he so recognized, had already been influenced by custom. He tells us that Cicero's *Hortensius*, which contained an exhortation to philosophy, had changed the direction of his mind.

> The book excited and inflamed me; in my ardor the only thing I found lacking was that the name of Christ was not there. *For*

with my mother's milk my infant heart had drunk in, and still held deep
down in it, that name according to your mercy, O Lord, the name of your
Son, my Savior, and whatever lacked that name, no matter how learned
and excellently written, could not win me wholly.[6]

When, however, he started to study the Scriptures, "they
seemed to me", he says, "unworthy to be compared with the
majesty of Cicero", an author who wrote in the style to which
he was accustomed.[7]

The proper words to describe our assent or dissent in relation to a given intellectual discourse because of our habituation
will be (even though we may be unaware of them) "I like what
I hear, it is what I'm used to hearing", and "I do not like what
I hear, I'm not used to hearing it." Such is the case when we
base our acceptance or rejection, not upon evidence and the
ability to consider reasonably what we hear, but upon our appetite, which moves us to respond as we do.

We can, I think, clarify and give substance to the role of
appetite in the intellectual life if we pay attention to some distinctions we learn from Saint Thomas. He teaches us that the
intellect moves the will in the species of final cause—nothing
is desired unless it is presented by the intellect and seems good
—while the will moves the intellect in the species of agent
cause, for the will is the moving cause of all the powers of the
soul except the vegetative.[8]

This latter dependency, of the intellect upon the will, applied more properly to the speculative intellect, leads, as Saint
Thomas shows, to a further distinction.[9] The speculative intellect is dependent upon the will in two ways. Thinking is,
first of all, natural and seems good to the will; and so the intellect thinks and, in thinking, can sometimes come to *know*.
In this case the *thinking* depends upon the will, but not the
knowledge, for it comes from the evidence of the object; it is
the object that determines the intellect to think as it does.

Sometimes, however, the will moves the intellect to accept
as true something for which it has no evidence. Here, not only
does the activity of thinking depend upon the will, but *what*

the intellect thinks as well. What the intellect thinks about the object is determined by the will.

We can make, again with Saint Thomas, some further clarifications.[10] Our intellect is in potency to all intelligible forms, as is prime matter to all sensible forms. It is not in the beginning more determined one way than another. Anything that is indeterminate in this way is *brought* to a determination. The possible intellect must therefore be moved, and it will be so moved, granted the first movement of thinking, either by the object it thinks about or by the will. When, faced with an object, it is not more disposed to accept one part of a contradiction rather than another, the intellect will be in a state of *doubt*. When it adheres more to one part of a contradiction than to another, with fear that the other might be true, there will be *opinion*. When the intellect is determined to one part of a contradiction without fear that the other might be true, there will be *understanding*, through immediate evidence, or *science*, if of a conclusion depending upon immediate evidence.

When, however, the will moves the intellect to accept something determinately, not because it apprehends it as knower, but solely because it seems good, there will be *faith*.

> In this situation [says Saint Thomas] our understanding is determined by the will, which chooses to assent to one side [of a contradiction] definitely and precisely because of something which is enough to move the will, though not enough to convince the understanding—namely, since it seems good or fitting to assent to this side. And this is the state of one who believes what another says because it seems fitting or useful to do so.

The object of faith is not manifest. The will, therefore, does not add to the object as *true*; the intellect adheres to the object because it seems good to the will. The intellect in this case is held captive by the will.

When the intellect is moved by the will to posit an act of human faith, it is never certain of attaining the truth. All the intellect has are signs, which are many times precarious. Such

signs in the intellectual life are: (a) the reputation of a teacher;
(b) the fact that what he says is a reaffirmation of what one
has heard before, (c) the fact that what he says fits with an
antecedent disposition.

We cannot avoid the role of human faith in the intellectual
life, because when we begin to think, the intellect is not capable
of judging what is proposed. We are, as it were, *born* into the
intellectual life, and before the intellect can reasonably assent
to anything, it has heard all sorts of opinions and untethered
statements, and it is moved to judge according to what it has
heard before, rejecting what seems strange to it. The will, to
repeat, moves the intellect to represent to itself as a good (for
the *truth* is a good) that which it has heard in its *milieu*. This
is a determination of the intellect before the intellect poses a
genuine act of knowledge. The intellect is determined by the
fluctuations of the milieu in which it has participated, which
custom imposes, a determination with which it comes to the
intellectual life.

There is then an *Intellectual Mos*, in both senses of the word
with which we began: *a natural or quasi-natural inclination of the
intellect*, of which the will is the principle, in dependence upon
the time and *custom* within which it exists.

II

Man, by nature a social and political animal, is not meant to
live alone. He needs others, *which he uses as if they were himself.*
This is easily seen in any society, where among other depen-
dencies, he takes, because of his ignorance, what others say *as
if what is said were known to him.* Without a trust in the words
of others, human society would be impossible, and it is for
this reason that Cicero teaches that truthfulness is a part of
justice,[11] a doctrine with which Saint Thomas agrees.[12] There
are good customs; without them we would be "the worst of
animals". There are also bad customs, and we would rid our-

selves of them if we could; the only way, however, would be by substitution, for it is impossible to live without some custom.

Because the human intellect is weak, and because the pure life of intelligence is, properly, a divine life, there is a necessity of first believing before we *can* acquire knowledge or even good opinion. Saint Thomas gives witness by reflecting upon the order of disciplines in relation to our order of knowing. While metaphysics is the highest natural wisdom, which considers being as being and the first principle of being, and while it confirms and defends the other disciplines, it is yet learned last. Along the way, however, the learner will accept on faith that the order of learning and the things he learns will lead, finally, to the apprehension of God as the first principle of all reality. He will also believe some truths from outside the first disciplines he learns, which only later will he understand. He will not be able to defend even the first principles of the disciplines he learns until he studies metaphysics, which defends itself and all the other disciplines.

The unwillingness to submit to intellectual masters condemns the intellect to wander aimlessly and without profit, a wandering that seems nevertheless to bespeak an autonomy freed from the slavery of a mindless repetition of old and irrelevant doctrines hardened into dogmas. The autonomy is an illusion. Gilson has well shown, for example, how Descartes, in attempting to rethink the whole philosophical enterprise, to free himself from every influence, yet uses scholastic terms and expressions, even though transformed, which he no doubt received from his Catholic teachers. When, therefore, Rousseau, in his *Discourse on the Sciences and Arts*, admits finally that some few thinkers might be necessary for the well-being of mankind, he yet restricts severely their number to those "whom nature destined to be her disciples", who "need[ed] no teachers":

> Verulam [Bacon], Descartes, Newton, these preceptors of the human race, had none themselves; indeed, what guides would have led them as far as their vast genius carried them? Ordinary teachers would only have restricted their understanding by

confining it within the narrow capacity of their own. The first obstacles taught them to exert themselves, and they did their utmost to traverse the immense space they covered. If a few men must be allowed to devote themselves to the study of the sciences and arts, it must be only those who feel the strength to walk alone in their footsteps and go beyond them.[13]

While there might be some truth in Rousseau's position, it is fair to note that Euclid's *Elements* played an immense role in Newton's *Principia* and Descartes' *Geometrie* and that Bacon would have been hard pressed to write about his idols without the benefit of previous thinkers or to determine clearly his method without comparing it to a version of the Aristotelian tradition he hoped to displace. And all were probably taught to read and write, and thought and wrote using the customary grammar of their languages. No one escapes the effect of intellectual custom, no matter how far he extends the province of learning or how much he opposes his predecessors. (This is the inescapable truth that leads some to the conclusion that no doctrine can even be understood without knowing the times in which it was written, itself a doctrine that makes liberal education impossible.) "We stand", says Saint Bernard, "on the shoulders of giants", whose doctrines were no doubt understood only after having been believed to be worthy of a most serious attention.

Saint Augustine saw clearly the universal importance of custom in the intellectual life. He teaches that there is a natural order of learning. He asks where, in his argument with the Manichees, he should begin:

Where, then, shall I begin? With authority or with reasoning? *In the order of nature*, when we learn anything, authority precedes reasoning. For a reason may seem weak, when, after it is given, it requires authority to confirm it. But because the minds of men are obscured by familiarity with darkness, which covers them in the night of sins and evil habits, and cannot perceive in a way suitable to the clearness and purity of reason, there is a most wholesome provision for bringing the dazzled eye into the light

of truth under the congenial shade of authority. But since we
have to do with people who are perverse in all their thoughts
and words and actions, and who insist on nothing more than
a beginning with argument, I will, *as a concession to them*, take
what I think the wrong method in discussion.[14]

Augustine uses this same doctrine in his sermons and letters:

If you cannot understand, believe in order that you may understand.[15]

What soul, hungering for eternity and shocked by the short-
ness of this present life, would resist the splendor and the majesty
of the authority of God?[16]

While Augustine is, in his sermons and epistles, speaking
about the supernatural truth and God's own authority, what
he says about the beginning of intellectual assent is true, as he
says, about the whole life of the intellect, especially in the case
of fallen man.

Newman is a further witness. He says:

I have no intention at all of denying that truth is the real object
of our reason, and that, if it does not attain the truth, either the
premise or the process is in fault; but I am not speaking of right
reason, but reason as it acts in fact and concretely in fallen man
and that its tendency is towards a simple unbelief in matters of
religion.[17]

He also speaks of the efforts "to withstand and baffle the
fierce energy of passion and the all-corroding, all-dissolving
skepticism of the intellect in religious inquiries."

If the intellectual custom that surrounds us is good, the intellect has a chance to become directed toward the truth, a chance
to lead a properly intellectual life. If, however, the custom is
bad, the intellect will be misdirected from the beginning, and
its chance of following the right path is close to nonexistent.

As in all things human, much of intellectual custom is not
helpful, and some of it is destructive. Eric Voeglin, in *The
New Science of Politics*, written years ago, gives us a sense of the
culture that surrounds us.

We live in the world of the dialogue,

where the recognition of the structure of reality, the cultivation
of the virtues of sophia and prudentia, the discipline of the intellect and the development of theoretical culture and the life
of spirit are stigmatized in public as reactionary, while disregard
for the structure of reality, ignorance of facts, fallacious miscon-
struction and falsification of history, irresponsible opining on
the basis of sincere conviction, philosophical illiteracy, spiritual
dullness, and agnostic sophistication are considered the virtues
of man, and their possession opens the road to public success.[18]

Since custom induces a second nature, the case of the corrupted intellect is all but hopeless. The intellect, once directed
against the truth, can, by natural means, hardly ever be sal-
vaged. This need not be because of a closed mind or bad morals,
though they play their part, but because of custom itself, which
incapacitates the intellect for the arduous task of pursuing wisdom. All this, the result of our fallen nature, makes a great
part of the intellectual life for most of us a matter of appetite.
Socrates is surely our friend when he so instructs us in the
Dialogues.

Since we cannot escape intellectual custom, and since most
intellectual customs are at the very least deficient, we are indeed in a precarious position with regard to the intellectual
life . . . and there seems to be no way through our difficulties.
(The attempt to doubt everything, so fashionable in our times,
is no solution, for then the intellectual life could never begin.)

III

Saint Paul admonishes Timothy, a bishop he himself had con-
secrated, to "preach the word, be urgent in season and out of
season, convince, rebuke, and exhort, be unfailing in patience
and in teaching" (2 Tim 4:2). He admonishes Titus, another
bishop, that he "must hold firm to the sure word as taught,
so that he may be able to give instruction to those who con-

tradict it" (Titus 1:9). It is most important, in every case, as Saint Paul charges Timothy, to "guard the truth that has been entrusted to you by the Holy Spirit who dwells within us" (2 Tim 1:14).

The Church has, as part of her mission, the duty to teach, explain, conserve, and defend the revelation which has been entrusted to her in Scripture and tradition. Because we to whom that revelation is offered could never arrive, by reason alone, at the most important truths it teaches, because it is supereminently truthful, and because it does not attempt to defend its truths, it should not be surprising that the content of Divine teaching has been so often the subject of dispute, and that it has been obscured, distorted, and even denied by those who claim to believe it. It must be clarified, "in season and out of season", if it is to be conserved, and the errors that would destroy it must be from time to time exposed and anathematized. So difficult is it to understand *what exactly* God is teaching through his revelation, so prone is the human intellect to fashion fables in its place, so easy is it to misunderstand with the best of intentions, and so contrary to it are the customs of the world, that Saint Augustine was prompted to say that heresies are good for the Church because they lead to fruitful clarifications, without which the teachings of the faith would most probably become more vague with the passage of time.

The Church teaches us through councils, definitions, encyclicals, apostolic exhortations, the motu proprio, and so on. More to our point, the deposit of faith is also clarified, developed, and defended by sacred theology, and since theology is the work of human reason, even though illumined by faith, and is as such fallible, the Church, in fulfilling her mission, judges theological doctrines and guides us here as elsewhere. This very guidance is, in fact, based, as are all the prerogatives of the Magisterium, upon the promises of Christ that the Church would never fail in proclaiming the truth and in helping us to adhere to it.

In so judging theological doctrines, *the Church establishes an intellectual custom that is opposed to the fluctuations, weaknesses, and perversities of human custom; it is based upon God's word and the inspiration of the Holy Spirit, and it can never deceive.*

In following the teaching of the Church here as elsewhere, we are more certain of being in the path of truth than we are of any purely human truth we can ever hold. Remember, in this connection, that what we hold by human faith is less certain than opinion or science and unsatisfactory so far as the intellect is concerned. It is greatly different with supernatural faith. Though the intellect as such is not satisfied even when we hold something by Divine faith, we are, because we rest on God's own intellect and because we are moved by him to accept his teaching, more certain here than we are in holding anything by reason alone.

What, then, does the Church, to whom he has entrusted his concerns for us, teach concerning theological doctrines?

1. Pope John XXII, speaking about Saint Thomas, said before his canonization that "his life was saintly and his doctrine could only be miraculous . . . because he enlightened the church more than all the other doctors. By the use of his works a man could profit more in one year than if he studies the doctrine of others for his whole life."

2. Saint Pius V declared him a Doctor of the Church, saying he was "the most brilliant light of the Church", whose works are "the most certain rule of Christian doctrine by which he enlightened the Apostolic Church in answering conclusively numberless errors . . . which illumination has often been evident in the past and recently stood forth prominently in the decrees of the Council of Trent."

3. Benedict XIII wrote to the Order of Preachers that they should "pursue with energy your Doctor's works, more brilliant than the sun and written without the shadow of error. These works made the Church illustrious with wonderful erudition, since they march ahead and proceed with unimpeded step, protecting and vindicating by the surest rule of Christian doctrine, the truth of our holy religion."

4. Leo XIII stated that "this is the greatest glory of Thomas, altogether his own and shared with no other Catholic Doctor, that the Fathers of Trent, in order to proceed in an orderly fashion during the conclave, desired to have opened upon the altar together with the Scriptures and the decrees of the Supreme Pontiffs, the *Summa* of Saint Thomas Aquinas whence they could draw counsel, reasons, and answers."

Again from Leo XIII: "This point is vital, that Bishops expend every effort to see that young men destined to be the hope of the Church should be imbued with the holy and heavenly doctrine of the Angelic Doctor. In those places where young men have devoted themselves to the patronage and doctrine of Saint Thomas, true wisdom will flourish, drawn as it is from solid principles and explained by reason in an orderly fashion   Theology proceeding correctly and well according to the plan and method of Aquinas is in accordance with our command. Every day We become more clearly aware how powerfully Sacred Doctrine taught by its master and patron, Thomas, affords the greatest possible utility for both clergy and laity."

5. Saint Pius X said that the chief of Leo's achievements is his restoration of the doctrine of Saint Thomas. For he "restored the Angelic Doctor . . . as the leader and master of theology, whose divine genius fashioned weapons marvelously suited to protect the truth and destroy the many errors of the times. Indeed those principles of wisdom, useful for all time, which the holy Doctors passed on to us, have been organized by no one more aptly than by Thomas, and no one has explained them more clearly." Indeed, Pius said, those who depart from the teaching of Saint Thomas "seem to effect ultimately their withdrawal from the Church. . . . As we have said, one may not desert Aquinas, especially in philosophy and theology, without great harm; following him is the safest way to the knowledge of divine things. . . . If the doctrine of any other author or saint has ever been approved at any time by us or our predecessors with singular commendation joined with an invitation and

order to propagate and to defend it, it may be easily understood
that it was commended only insofar as it agreed with the principles of Aquinas or was in no way opposed to them." Theology
professors "should also take particular care that their students
develop a deep affection for the *Summa.* . . . In this way and no
other will theology be restored to its pristine dignity, and the
proper order and value will be restored to all sacred studies,
and the province of the intellect and reason flower again in a
second spring."

6. Benedict XV stated that "the eminent commendations of
Thomas Aquinas by the Holy See no longer permit a Catholic
to doubt that he was divinely raised up that the Church might
have a master whose doctrine should be followed in a special
way at all times."

7. Pius XI said that "indeed, We so approve of the tributes
paid to his almost divine brilliance that we believe Thomas
should be called not only Angelic but Common or Universal Doctor of the Church. As innumerable documents of every kind attest, the Church has adopted his doctrine for her
own. . . . It is no wonder that the Church has made this light
her own and has adorned herself with it, and has illustrated
her immortal doctrine with it. . . . It is no wonder that all the
popes have vied with one another in exalting him, proposing
him, inculcating him, as a model, master, doctor, patron, and
protector of all schools. . . . Just as it was said of old to the
Egyptians in time of famine: 'Go to Joseph', so that they should
receive a supply of corn to nourish their bodies, so to those
who are now in quest of truth We now say: 'Go to Thomas'
that they may ask from him the food of solid doctrine of which
he has an abundance to nourish their souls unto eternal life."

Since sacred theology uses philosophy as a handmaid, the
Church's duty does not end with a judgment upon theology
alone but extends to philosophy as well.

1. Pius XII said that "the Angelic Doctor interpreted [Aris-
totle] in a uniquely brilliant manner. He made that philosophy
Christian when he purged it of the errors into which a pagan

writer would easily fall; he used those very errors in his exposition and vindication of Catholic truth. Among the important advances which the Church owes to the great Aquinas this certainly should be included that so nicely did he harmonize Christian truth with the enduring peripatetic philosophy that he made Aristotle cease to be an adversary and become, instead, a militant supporter for Christ. . . . Therefore, those who wish to be true philosophers . . . should take the principles and foundations of their doctrine from Thomas Aquinas. To follow his leadership is praiseworthy: on the contrary, to depart foolishly and rashly from the wisdom of the Angelic Doctor is something far from Our mind and fraught with peril. . . . For those who apply themselves to the teaching and study of theology and philosophy should consider it their capital duty, having set aside the findings of a fruitless philosophy, to follow Saint Thomas Aquinas and to cherish him as their master and their leader."

2. Saint Pius X said that "all who teach philosophy in Catholic schools throughout the world should take care never to depart from the path and method of Aquinas, and to insist upon that procedure more vigorously every day. . . . We warn teachers to keep this religiously in mind, especially in metaphysics, that to disregard Aquinas cannot be done without suffering great harm."

3. Benedict XV said that "along with our predecessors We are equally persuaded that the only philosophy worth our efforts is that which is according to Christ. Therefore the study of philosophy according to the principles and system of Aquinas must certainly be encouraged so that the explanation and invincible defense of divinely revealed truth may be as full as human reason can make of it."

These are but a few of the testimonies of the popes throughout the centuries after the death of Saint Thomas, and I could have added the testimony of John Paul II, but that would have entailed repeating almost wholly two separate addresses, one on the philosophy of Thomas Aquinas to the Angelicum University, the other to the Eighth International Thomistic Congress, wherein the Holy Father repeats for the most part the commendations of his predecessors concerning the doctrine, principles, and method of Saint Thomas and emphasizes the importance of adhering to him today for the facing of modern problems both theological and philosophical.

IV

It is, of course decisive for us to believe that we can never be deceived by the teaching Church. Since, however, the supernatural life is based upon the natural, and is never in opposition to it, since grace perfects nature, it would be strange if, believing and practicing our faith, we did not in the course of our lives experience in some sense a ring of truth the more we conform to the norms of the Magisterium. It would be strange, for instance, if living according to the sexual morality of the gospel we did not experience, amidst all the attendant difficulties, a sense of joy, a peace of conscience, and the inner freedom that results from self-control. The same is true in the intellectual life; it would be strange if in following the Church's guidance, we did not experience a sense of accomplishment, a sense that we were progressing, a sense that we were, as we go on, more at one with the reality that is the object of our study.

Such is in fact the case with the study of Saint Thomas.

To have found a master in the intellectual life is as precious as it is rare; to have been directed to one by the Church is as fortunate as it is precious.

It was reported that Saint Thomas himself "no sooner heard [Saint Albert] expound every science with such wondrous depth of wisdom, than he rejoiced exceedingly at having quickly found that which he had come to seek, one who offered him so unsparingly the fulfillment of his heart's desire." It is said further that, in order to profit from this exceptional opportunity, he "began to be more than ever silent, more than ever assiduous in study and devout in prayer."[19]

Saint Thomas himself gives us an insight into the importance of a good teacher. He shows that something may be in potency in two ways. Air, to take an example, is in potency to be consumed by fire passively; if fire is to spread, fire itself will be the principal agent, extrinsic to the air it consumes. On the other hand, a living thing is in potency to health actively; if there is to be health, the living thing itself is the principal agent, and any extrinsic agents, such as the doctor, are secondary agents helping the principal agent achieve its end.

The intellect is in potency to science, and its potency is active. Just as a living thing, becoming sick, can become healthy by nature or by the help of secondary agents, so the intellect can learn through discovery or, most likely, with the help of a teacher. Where there is a teacher, the intellect of the learner is always the principal cause of learning; the teacher is never more than a secondary cause. Just as the doctor must follow the order of nature if he expects to heal, so the teacher must, says Saint Thomas, follow the order the intellect would follow without him if it could. This means that the teacher must follow the order of discovery, the order that is natural to the intellect, if he is to teach. If he does not follow the order imposed by the object of study, he becomes a cause of the corruption of the learner's mind, even though he says what is true.

This can be seen, says Saint Thomas, by reflecting upon the means the human teacher must use as he teaches. Unlike God, who can illumine the intellect from within, or an angel, who can order the imagination from within, the human teacher uses words as signs, which are proposed to the learner from *without*. The order in the teacher's words reflect the order of his concepts. The more orderly the words, the more orderly the concepts. The learner hears the words of the teacher, and they lead to images in his imagination; the more orderly are those words, the more orderly are the images; the more orderly the images, the more orderly the concepts in his intellect, which are abstracted from the images.

So weak is the human intellect—unlike the body, which does not need the doctor for the most part—that, as Saint Thomas says, *the words of the teacher are more proportioned to the intellect than things themselves*. Since we learn through the use of images, and words can bring about an ordering of those images, the great teacher, through the excellence of his words, orders well the images in our imagination, and through them our minds, with the result that we can be led to understand the realities signified by the words. *The more we apply ourselves to the words, and hence the concepts of the master, the more will we grasp reality*. And since, as learners, we are ignorant, and since truth is difficult to obtain, we must have faith enough in the teacher to stay with his words, through them to grasp his thought, and through that thought to become one with the objects themselves. We can see from the very nature of teaching and learning that without faith, learning becomes almost impossible; no faith, no light.

Saint Thomas proves to be the master who, without peer, can order our minds, so that we ordinary mortals can in our limited way come to see some of the truths we first accepted from him on faith, truths we would never have seen without that faith in the master.

It is then most important that here, as elsewhere, we obey the Church; if we do, we shall experience some of what she teaches about Saint Thomas, and we shall see for ourselves more about reality than ever we would had we studied without him.

NOTES

[1] *ST* I–II, 58, 1.

[2] II *Metaphysics* 3.

[3] I, 51.

[4] "Of Custom", in *Essays*, I, 23.

[5] *Confessions* 5, 14–15; emphases mine.

[6] Ibid., 3, 4; emphases mine.

[7] Ibid., 5.

[8] *ST* I, 82, 4.

[9] *De Virtutibus in Communi* 7.

[10] *De Veritate* 14, 1.

[11] *De Officiis* I, 7.

[12] *ST* II–II, 109, 3.

[13] Jean-Jacques Rousseau, *The First and Second Discourses*, ed. Roger D. Masters (New York: St. Martin's Press, 1964), 63.

[14] *De Moribus Ecclesiae* 2; emphases mine.

[15] *Sermo* 118.

[16] *Epistle* 137.

[17] *Apologia* 5.

[18] Eric Voeglin, *The New Science of Politics* (Chicago: University of Chicago Press, 1952), 178.

[19] James A. Weisheipl, O.P., *Friar Thomas D'Aquino: His Life, Thought, and Work* (Garden City, N.Y.: Doubleday, 1974), 44.

ABBREVIATIONS

Credo	*In Symbolum Apostolorum, scilicet, 'Credo in Deum' Expositio*
In Boe.	*In Librum Boethii de Trinitate*
QDV	*Questiones Disputate de Veritate*
SCG	*Summa Contra Gentiles*
Sent.	*Scriptum Super Sententiis*
ST	*Summa Theologiae*
Super Hebr.	*Super Epistolas S. Pauli ad Hebraeos*
Super Ioan.	*Super Evangelium S. Ioannis*
Super Rom.	*Super Epistolas S. Pauli ad Romanos*